Purifying the Altar

Purifying the Altar

Al Houghton

Word At Work Ministries, Inc.
Placentia, California

All scripture quotations, not otherwise indicated, are from *The New King James Version*: Copyright © 1982 by Thomas Nelson, Inc. Used by permission.

Biblical definitions from the *Theological Dictionary Of The New Testament* Volume II. Used by permission of Wm. B. Eerdmans Publishing Co.

Biblical definitions from the *Lexical Aids To Both The New And Old Testament* as published in the Hebrew Greek Key Study Bible. I highly recommend this edition for every believer. It can be purchased from AMG Publishers, Chattanooga, TN 37422.

Scriptures taken from the *Holy Bible, New International Version*. Copyright © 1973, 1978, 1984 International Bible Society. Used by permission of Zondervan Bible Publishers.

Definition taken from *American Dictionary Of The English Language, Noah Webster 1828*. Noah Webster's First Edition Of An American Dictionary Of The English Language. Published by the Foundation For American Christian Education. Copyright 1967.

The Expositor's Greek Testament. Published by William B. Eerdman's Publishing Co., 255 Jefferson SE, Grand Rapids, MI 49503. Reprinted September 1983.

The Amplified Bible. Zondervan Corporation, Grand Rapids, Michigan 49506 Copyright © 1965.

Purifying the Altar
Published by:
Word At Work Ministries, Inc.
P. O. Box 366 Placentia, CA 92670
ISBN: 0-940252-01-5

Second Printing, November 1995

Printed in the United States of America.

Dedication

This book is gratefully dedicated to my family. Jayne, my wife, has extended grace and patience during the many extra hours given to a manuscript instead of her.

Jonathan, Julie, and Michael have been equally understanding of the days and hours away from home where God birthed the principles shared in these pages!

Contents

Chapter 1
What Is An Altar?

When a New Testament believer hears the word "altar," the first image which usually comes to mind is one of animal sacrifice. While animal sacrifices were a definite part of what happened at some of the altars in the Old Testament, there was a much larger dimension of spiritual activity. The patriarchs built their own altars, and almost always erected one to commemorate an event in which they had met with God. Altars commemorated receiving a revelation, a promise, or making vows.

After the flood, Noah had some serious business to discuss with the Lord.

> So Noah went out, and his sons and wife and his sons' wives with him.
>
> Every beast, every creeping thing, every bird, and whatever creeps on the earth, according to their families, went out of the ark.
>
> Then Noah built an altar to the Lord, and took of every clean animal and of every clean bird, and offered burnt offerings on the altar.
>
> And the Lord smelled a soothing aroma. Then the Lord said in His heart, "I will never again curse the ground for man's sake, although the imagination of man's heart is evil from his youth; nor will I again destroy every living thing as I have done.
>
> "While the earth remains, seedtime and harvest, And cold

and heat, And winter and summer, And day and night Shall not cease."

Genesis 8:18-22

We are still enjoying the blessing of the promise God gave Noah. The law of seedtime and harvest still works. Without it, we could not buy what we want from the grocery store. God gave covenant promises, direction, and blessing to one who worshipped at an altar.

The Father reveals Himself in the Old Testament as the God of Abraham, Isaac, and Jacob. The sum and substance of His dealing, maturing, and revealing always produced the same response. It was in those places the patriarchs built an altar.

Famous Altars

Abram built several altars, but perhaps the most famous was the one on which he prepared to sacrifice his son. When asked by Isaac, "Where is the lamb?" he received a revelation of the ministry of Jesus, and said, "God will provide Himself the lamb for a burnt offering." This revelation came at an altar!

Years later, when Moses received the Law at Mt. Sinai, God gave specific plans for two altars. The brazen altar was the very first thing every worshipper saw when entering the Tabernacle, because it was placed in the outer court, right in front of the entrance. It signified man had no access to God except as a sinner atoned for through the shedding of blood!

The second altar was in the Holy Place, right in front of the veil which marked the entrance of the Holy of Holies. To walk into God's presence, you had to pass the altar of incense and walk through the veil.

This altar taught enjoying the real presence of God is only available to the true worshippers who praise and worship from a pure heart. Worship truly is the doorway to His presence, while the veil is our flesh. When we determine to praise and worship regardless of how we feel, the door opens to God's presence! The first Tabernacle was a physical picture of the importance of altars in doing business with God.

When Naaman the Syrian obeyed the prophet's command, healing came with a revelation of the true God! Once the true was recognized, the next order of business was obtaining a pure place where he could worship. Second Kings 5:15-17 says:

> Then he returned to the man of God, he and all his aides, and came and stood before him; and he said, "Indeed, now I know that there is no God in all the earth, except in Israel; now therefore, please take a gift from your servant."
>
> But he said, "As the Lord lives, before whom I stand, I will receive nothing." And he urged him to take it, but he refused.
>
> So Naaman said, "Then, if not, please let your servant be given two mule-loads of earth; for your servant will no longer offer either burnt offering or sacrifice to other gods, but to the Lord.

Naaman was determined to no longer deal with the counterfeit, because he had found the real! I believe this story bears great prophetic truth for every generation of the Body of Christ as it transitions from one season to the next! The two mule-loads of earth would form his altar upon which to approach his newfound God with thanksgiving!

Men's Hearts Revealed

The Lord revealed integrity of heart. Naaman's heart was also revealed. He refused to worship any other God but the Lord. Elisha's heart was revealed. He had the opportunity to profit from the anointing accompanying his office, but refused. Gehazi's heart was revealed. He chose to fund-raise, manipulate, and profit from God's anointing.

I believe, once again, God is revealing hearts!

Those who have Gehazi's heart will find the leprosy of judgment clinging to them. Gehazi became an example for all to see of what happens to those who set their heart on money! The attitude characterized by Gehazi makes an altar impure!

Several years ago I was given a copy of *An American Dictionary Of The English Language*, published by Noah Webster in 1828, before humanistic scholarship edited out our Christian faith. A high percentage of the definitions have biblical backgrounds. The definition of "altar" is extremely interesting:

1. A mount; a table or elevated place, on which sacrifices were anciently offered to some deity.

2. In modern churches, the communion table; and, figuratively, a church.

3. In scripture, Christ is called the altar of Christians, He being the atoning sacrifice for sin.

I like Webster's second definition, "In modern churches, the communion table; and, figuratively, a church." When we talk about "purifying the altar," we are talking about accepting God's purpose, correction, and reproof and walking with Him accordingly in our homes, businesses, and churches.

The purpose of this book, *Purifying the Altar*, deals with transformation of the heart from self-seeking to servanthood, and from tradition to deliverance. Both self-seeking and tradition are elements that hinder God's purpose, while lying under the surface seemingly undetected.

Just as God met with Abraham, Isaac, and Jacob to direct, mature, correct, and lead them toward His perfect will and plan, so He meets with us for the same purpose. The sum and substance of His dealings are the fruit of the time we spend at our personal and corporate altars.

If an individual altar is pure, but joined to a corporate (church or ministry) altar that is impure, the second will dramatically affect the first. God's intent has always been for the pure corporate (church or ministry) altar to positively influence the individual.

When the integrity of the corporate altar was corrupted,

God always sent correction as a covenant blessing. The correction was not always received, but even in rejection, motivation of heart was visibly made manifest!

Will the real Gehazis please stand up!

Chapter 2
The Half-Truth Lie

Repent therefore and be converted, that your sins may be blotted out, so that times of refreshing may come from the presence of the Lord,

And that He may send Jesus Christ, who was preached to you before,

whom heaven must receive until the times of restoration of all things, which God has spoken by the mouth of all His holy prophets since the world began.

Acts 3:19-21

This scripture guarantees Jesus will personally supervise the restoration of the Church in the last days, fulfilling every prophetic word ever spoken and recorded by His prophets in the Bible!

The Church must not only become one without spot, wrinkle, or blemish, but an effective army bringing in a worldwide harvest!

Isaiah spoke of the Church as spiritual Israel in Isaiah 60:1,2.

Arise, shine; For your light has come! And the glory of the Lord is risen upon you.

For behold, the darkness shall cover the earth, And deep darkness the people; But the Lord will arise over you, And His glory will be seen upon you.

Isaiah 60:1,2

Isaiah is prophesying visible manifestations of God's blessing that must be seen as a testimony of His grace!

The Gentiles shall come to your light, and kings to the brightness of your rising.

Lift up your eyes all around, and see: they all gather together, they come to you; your sons shall come from afar, and your daughters shall be nursed at your side.

Then you shall see and become radiant, And your heart shall swell with joy; Because the abundance of the sea shall be turned to you, The wealth of the Gentiles shall come to you.

Isaiah 60:3-5

Isaiah prophesied a dramatic transfer of wealth from Satan's control to God's. Has this promise been fulfilled in the restoration of *all* things?

God's Provision for Harvest

This transfer appears to be a two-edged sword. One edge is a judgment on the materialistic world while the other is God's provision for an end-time harvest, but definitely not for personal promotion or satisfying soulish craving.

In Isaiah 61:6 the Lord says, "You shall eat the riches of the Gentiles, and in their glory you shall boast."

Worldly people glory and boast in their wealth. Is the Church being prepared for a transfer?

Verse 7 says:

Instead of your shame you shall have double honor, And instead of confusion they shall rejoice in their portion. Therefore in their land they shall possess double....

It appears God is once again giving by promise that which must be possessed. Just like the children of Israel coming out of Egypt had to possess the land of promise, so we must possess our Caanan. God gave it by promise, but it was possessed by anointing, perseverance, courage, wisdom, and obedience.

Not everyone who came out of Egypt made it into Caanan. Many fell by the wayside. It was not God's best for them, but it happened.

The Father wants us to go in and possess what He has promised. Sovereignly, God will move for those He has chosen. He has no accidents. I believe we were born and live in this season because God foreordained our participation in an enormous end-time revival.

The foundation for God's blessing is made possible through covenant. It can only be appropriated and dispensed through covenant.

Malachi 3:8-10 alludes to the foundation of our covenant:

Will a man rob God? Yet you have robbed Me! But you say, "In what way have we robbed You?" In tithes and offerings.

You are cursed with a curse, For you have robbed Me, Even this whole nation.

Bring all the tithes into the storehouse, That there may be food in My house, And prove Me now in this, Says the Lord of hosts, If I will not open for you the windows of heaven And pour out for you such blessing That there will not be room enough to receive it.

The magnitude of this promise is punctuated by a unique challenge. God had said, "Thou shalt not tempt the Lord thy God," but here He says, "Put Me to the test. Prove Me now in this. I dare you!"

If you tithe, do you have such blessing there is not room enough to contain it? Are the windows of heaven open to you to the degree this passage promises? Are the windows of heaven open to the Body of Christ as a whole? Many of us can point to people who are blessed in measure, but are the windows really open to the extent promised?

God claims the earth and everything in it by right of creation, including the silver, gold, and cattle on a thousand hills. In addition, He reserves the right to do whatever He wants with it. The covenant clearly indicates He wants to bless His people, but we must do our part.

This passage has been interpreted for us in a very traditional way, and every minister who goes to Bible school or seminary usually learns the traditional understanding and preaches it accordingly.

As I began to seek the Lord as to why the windows were *not* open to the saints, certain surprising insights began to come! For the first time I saw impurity and manipulation in our traditional way of preaching the tithe. Our first error of tradition was in emphasizing a half-truth. We emphasized a believer's decision to tithe as the key guaranteeing God will open the windows of heaven.

Preaching a Half-Truth

We generally preached it this way: "If you will make the decision to tithe, God will open the windows of heaven for you." We placed the entire responsibility on each believer. By saying, "If you will tithe, God will open the windows of heaven for you," we preached a half-truth, because there is more involved. Half-truth can quickly degenerate into untruth.

The other side of the coin would say, "If the windows are not open, the fault is with you!" The scenario has unfolded progressively. We preach, "If you tithe, God will...," but God hasn't in promised measure; therefore, where are we missing God's promises?

We need to understand covenant! Marriage is an example of covenant. No one can marry himself. A covenant is a mutual agreement between two *separate* parties. You cannot have a covenant unless two individuals agree.

The language of Malachi 3 speaks of covenant. When two people come to terms in covenant, and as each diligently adheres to those terms, the agreement is consummated.

God has offered a fundamental monetary covenant to His people, but it is obvious from the financial condition of the saints that the covenant is not being fully consummated.

In every congregation in North America, the majority of people who tithe will agree, "We tithe and are doing the best we know to do, but we do not see the windows of heaven opened to the full extent God promised." The real question is, why? Assuming it is not God's fault, we must ask ourselves, "Where are we missing it?"

Jesus referred to a potential answer when He said in Mark 7:13, "Your traditions have made the word of God of none effect." Is it possible our teaching of the tithe in the traditional way, as we learned it in Bible school, has made the Word of God of none effect, closing rather than opening the windows of heaven? I believe this is the case.

Jesus clearly exposed our first tradition in Matthew 23:13-19, when He said:

> But woe to you, scribes and Pharisees, hypocrites! For you *shut up* the kingdom of heaven against men; for you neither go in yourselves, nor do you allow those who are entering to go in.
>
> Woe to you, scribes and Pharisees, hypocrites! For you devour widows' houses, and for a pretense make long prayers. Therefore you will receive greater condemnation.
>
> Woe to you, scribes and Pharisees, hypocrites! For you travel land and sea to win one proselyte, and when he is won, you make him twice as much a son of hell as yourselves.
>
> Woe to you, blind guides, who say, "Whoever swears by the temple, it is nothing; but whoever swears by the gold of the temple, he is obliged to perform it."
>
> Fools and blind! For which is greater, the gold or the temple that sanctifies the gold?
>
> And, "Whoever swears by the altar, it is nothing; but whoever swears by the gift that is on it, he is obliged to perform it."
>
> Fools and blind! For which is greater, the *gift* or the *altar* that sanctifies the gift?

In our traditional teaching of the tithe, we have made the gift greater than the altar which sanctifies the gift.

By preaching the tithe in the traditional way, we have been able to build a steady financial base in our local churches without any obligation on our part to organizationally adhere to God's revealed plan. This gives leadership the freedom to do what they want to do, and places all the burden on the saints.

The fruit of our tradition is everywhere in manifestation. There is a distinct lack of open windows to God's people who tithe. There has been a measure of blessing, but it is probably based more on grace than obedience.

Which is greater, the gift or the altar that sanctifies the gift? Jesus said those of us who thought the gift was greater than the altar are fools and blind. According to Jesus, *the condition of the place where we give is more important than the giving*.

The Greek word translated "sanctify" is *hag-ee-ad-zo*. It means "to make, render or declare, sacred or holy, to consecrate." This word appears in The Lord's Prayer, "Hallowed be thy name..." It is translated in a number of places "sanctify, or sanctified." *Hag-ee-ad-zo* appears in Acts 20:32 in a context similar to Matthew 23.

And now, brethren, I commend you to God and to the word of His grace, which is able to build you up and give you an inheritance among all those who are *sanctified*.

Hag-ee-ad-zo here, as in Matthew 23, means "to separate from things profane and dedicate to God, to consecrate and so render inviolable."

When the tithe is put on a pure altar, it is made holy and acceptable to God; consequently, the covenant is completed. But the converse of that is also true. When the tithe is put on an impure altar, it is made unholy, and the covenant is not completed.

We have failed to understand a foundational principle: The purity of the altar *sanctifies* the gift. The condition of the altar determines the return on the giving! This is why Jesus started out by saying to the Pharisees, "You shut up the kingdom of heaven against men." How many leaders today are guilty of shutting the windows of heaven to the saints?

Jesus intimates the purity of the altar is more important than the tithe itself by saying, "Which is greater, the gift or the altar that sanctifies the gift?" For this covenant to be complete, each side must do its part to consummate the contract.

It is much more advantageous for those in leadership who want to do their own thing to emphasize the tithe without ever mentioning the condition of the altar. This mind-set leaves the leader free to do whatever seems good financially. But the fruit of the system is seen in the condition of the victims. The windows of heaven for many people seem closed. The context of Matthew 23 makes it very clear, Jesus is speaking about the tithe:

> **Woe to you, scribes and Pharisees, hypocrites! For you pay tithe of mint and anise and cummin, and have neglected the weightier matters of the law: justice and mercy and faith. These you ought to have done, without leaving the others undone.**

Jesus told them they had emphasized the tithe while neglecting other principles which ultimately affect the tithe. In effect, He said, "You have made the gift greater than the altar which sanctifies the gift, allowing you to do what you want financially but leaving people impoverished." This passage perfectly describes some of the fruit we have in Christendom today.

This understanding requires we deal with a variety of questions:

- What transpires in the realm of the spirit when we do business with God at an impure altar?
- What effect does the impurity have on the covenant?
- What makes an altar impure?
- How can we recognize an impure altar?
- What should we do to restore purity if, in fact, we discover the altar where we attend is impure?

In scripture, the altar was a place where man was led to do business with God; a place where God spoke to him and he responded with commitment. The altar was a place where the purpose and plan of God was received with commitment and dedication of heart.

The Old Testament altar and what transpired there is in many ways a type and a shadow of the business we should do with God in our New Testament churches. When we look at the purity of the altar, we are dealing with the purity of the local church.

First Kings chapters 12 and 13 give one example of impurity at the altar. God had spoken to Solomon about judgment as a result of his disobedience. But because of his father, David, Solomon would not see the judgment in his days; it would be deferred to his son's days.

Two Kingdoms

First Kings 12 is the account of Rehoboam, Solomon's son, taking charge of Israel, and God raising up an enemy named Jeroboam to fulfill the prophecy by taking ten of the twelve tribes, leaving Rehoboam with two.

Jeroboam's kingdom and the ten tribes became known as Israel, or the Northern Kingdom, and Rehoboam's two tribes became known as Judah, or the Southern Kingdom. The spirit of fear came on Jeroboam to move him beyond what God had commanded.

Then Jeroboam built Shechem in the mountains of Ephraim, and dwelt there. Also he went out from there and built Penuel.

And Jeroboam said in his heart, "Now the kingdom may return to the house of David (fear):

"If these people go up to offer sacrifices in the house of the Lord at Jerusalem, then the heart of this people will turn back to their lord, Rehoboam king of Judah, and they will kill me and go back to Rehoboam king of Judah."

> Therefore the king took counsel and made two calves of
> gold, and said to the people, "It is too much for you to go up
> to Jerusalem. Here are your gods, O Israel, which brought
> you up from the land of Egypt!"
>
> And he set up one in Bethel, and the other he put in Dan.
>
> Now this thing became a sin, for the people went to wor-
> ship before the one as far as Dan.
>
> 1 Kings 12:25-30

Jeroboam was afraid to let the Israelites go back to
Jerusalem to worship. He was afraid he would lose *control*.
In his mind, the only way to keep what God had given was
to start his own church. God had not commanded him to do
that. First Kings 12:31,32 states:

> He made shrines on the high places, and made priests
> from every class of people, who were *not of the sons of Levi.*
>
> Jeroboam ordained a feast on the fifteenth day of the
> eighth month, *like the feast that was in Judah,* and offered
> sacrifices on the altar. So he did at Bethel, sacrificing to the
> calves that he had made. And at Bethel he installed the
> priests of the high places which *he had made.*

In order to keep his own denomination going, Jeroboam
had to recruit priests, once again departing from God's
ordained plan. According to verse 32, he did his best to
duplicate the same meeting days and form of worship God
had set up for His people in Jerusalem.

A very interesting phrase begins to appear in verses 32
and 33. It is the phrase "he had made." It appears three
times, and distinctively points out the difference between man
doing something because he wants to, versus waiting and let-
ting God fulfill the divine plan. Verse 33 reveals the true
foundation of this altar.

> So he made offerings on the altar which *he had made* at
> Bethel on the fifteenth day of the eighth month, in the
> month which *he had devised* in his own heart. And he
> ordained a feast for the children of Israel, and offered sac-
> rifices on the altar and burned incense.

15

One of the ingredients which makes an altar pure or impure is the motivation of the individual who sets it up. Did God ordain the ministry or was it devised out of man's heart? How much of what is done there is from God, and how much is from man? What is the motivation for what is done, who is brought in, and what is preached? God's response toward impure altars is given in chapter 13:1,2:

> **And behold, a man of God went from Judah to Bethel by the word of the Lord, and Jeroboam stood by the altar to burn incense.**

> **Then he cried out against the altar by the word of the Lord, and said, "O altar, altar! Thus says the Lord: 'Behold, a child, Josiah by name, shall be born to the house of David; and on you he shall sacrifice the priests of the high places who burn incense on you, and men's bones shall be burned on you.'"**

The first law of the impure altar states that when a man devises in his own heart and raises up a ministry God has not ordained, he will die on the very altar he builds!

Seasons of this judgment usually fall in every generation. Spiritual death is far worse than physical death.

First Kings 13:3 is very distinctive, in that it shows the ashes poured out or going down. In some instances when sacrifices were offered on the altar and accepted by God, the fire fell from heaven, the aroma ascended to God, and it was accepted.

At an impure altar, instead of being accepted, the ashes are poured out or rejected. When we tithe into an impure altar, it is like pouring money into a hole! God is in no way obligated to bring the promised return, and the windows of heaven remain closed.

Impure altars never go unchallenged! The prophet came to speak the word of the Lord against the impurity of the altar, and the war was on. Jeroboam would much rather destroy the prophet than repent and destroy the altar. That attitude is still prevalent today, revealing hardness of heart.

When the king receives judgment in his own body as a reward for trying to destroy the prophet, it immediately changes his attitude. He wants his hand restored, so he asks the prophet to pray. When his hand is restored, the king asks the man of God to come home, promising to bless him and feed him, but the man of God says:

> **If you were to give me half your house, I would not go in with you; nor would I eat bread or drink water in this place.**
>
> **For so it was commanded me by the word of the Lord, saying, "You shall not eat bread, nor drink water, nor return by the same way you came."**

1 Kings 13:8,9

This speaks of a spiritual truth which is working whether we know it or not. Eating bread and drinking water is, of course, a type and a shadow of the spiritual bread and heavenly refreshing of the anointing which we desperately need in our lives. Its effect is to transform us as we receive from a pure altar — but when we participate in an impure altar, we receive something entirely different! The anointing imparted at a pure altar brings growth, maturity, and blessing, but the "anointing" imparted at an impure altar brings corruption and eventually destruction.

God commands the prophet to eat no bread and drink no water in that place. What condition is the place where you are spiritually eating and drinking?

Identifying With an Altar

Giving either tithe or offering fully and totally identifies us with the altar. By sowing seed into an altar, we are identified with that altar, for good and blessing or hurt and destruction!

> **"He who receives a prophet in the name of a prophet shall receive a prophet's reward."**

Matthew 10:41

If we are giving into an altar of impurity, that impurity

is transferred to us, and if we are giving to a pure altar, that purity becomes part of us. Jeroboam was very smart. He did not go to an out-of-the-way, unusual place, but to one that was acceptable, well known, and respected by people. Bethel was one place where God's house historically stayed.

This is a perfect example of how the devil operates today. Where does he work through deception to bring impurity? In the place where we all attend and know that God has ordained for us to grow and develop. The main attack is against the Church!

An old prophet who has been living in Bethel comes out to talk to the young prophet and tries to persuade him to come home and fellowship. The young prophet repeats the word of the Lord in verses 16-18.

> And he said, "I cannot return with you nor go in with you; neither can I eat bread or drink water with you in this place.
>
> "For I have been told by the word of the Lord, 'You shall not eat bread nor drink water there, nor return by going the way you came.'"
>
> He said to him, "I too am a prophet as you are, and an angel spoke to me by the word of the Lord, saying, 'Bring him back with you to your house, that he may eat bread and drink water.'" But he lied to him.

Does God contradict Himself? The young prophet went back and ate bread and drank water with the old prophet at Bethel. Verses 21 and 22 are even more revealing. The old prophet now speaks the authentic word of the Lord to the young prophet:

> ...Because you have disobeyed the word of the Lord, and have not kept the commandment which the Lord your God commanded you,
>
> but you came back, ate bread, and drank water in the place of which the Lord said to you, "Eat no bread and drink no water," your corpse shall not come to the tomb of your fathers.

The young prophet left. He was met by a lion and was

immediately killed. The lion stood there without moving; neither did it eat the body. This is a sign to the world that the spoken word of the Lord has been and would be fulfilled.

The first time I ever read this passage, I thought, "God, that is not fair." But sometimes in our humanistic society we need to remember God's kingdom operates on obedience.

I began to question how an old prophet could out of one side of his mouth lie convincingly and yet, just a few hours later, out of the other side of the same mouth, speak the word of the Lord. What turned the old prophet into an impure vessel?

An Impure Prophet

Undoubtedly the old prophet became like the altar at which he worshipped! He lived at Bethel. Was he a prophet? Yes, he was, but instead of moving to a pure altar, he stayed at a place where there was impurity. This produced mixed seed in his own life. On judgment day, he will give account for the life of the young prophet.

This should speak to us about the reason why we go where we go to church. Is it close? Is it conveniently located? Can we really afford decisions based on convenience? When we look at the eternal repercussions, convenience is absolutely the worse reason for going to a church and can, in fact, be the very leverage Satan uses to bring mixed seed into our lives. A little convenience here may breed a great deal of inconvenience throughout eternity!

The law of the altar states, *the condition of the altar where you attend, participate, and put your money is reproduced in your life, whether you are aware of it or not.* It is a spiritual law.

The old prophet could speak the word of the Lord, but because he had for a long time been in a place of impurity, he could *also* lie convincingly to get what he wanted. It was the same spirit which built the altar to start with. The lawlessness and willingness of Jeroboam to do whatever necessary to insure keeping what he wanted was transferred. The spirit of

Jeroboam which built the altar came into manifestation in the old prophet and cost the life of the young one.

Have you ever considered covenantal law dictates tithing could bring a curse instead of a blessing? In Malachi 2:1,2 God demands the priests honor His commandments and promises to those who refuse He will "curse" their "blessings." Keil and Delitzsch, a bastion of conservative scholarship, state in Vol. 10 pages 442, 443, "If they shall not do this, God will send the curse, against them, and that in two ways. In the first place He will curse their blessings; in fact, He has already done so. *Berakhoth*, blessings, are obviously not the revenues of the priests, tithes, atonement-money, and portions of the sacrifices (L. de Dieu, Ros., Hitzig), but the blessings pronounced by the priests upon the people by virtue of their office. These God will curse, i.e. He will make them ineffective, or turn them into the very opposite."

It is possible to write a check on Sunday morning and have God turn the prayer of blessing into a judgment of destruction! The condition of the altar determines blessing or curse.

Is the altar where you attend pure or impure, and what is the fruit of it in your life? Have lives been adversely affected by what has already been reproduced in you? How many lives have not been affected at all because nothing of value has been reproduced in you?

The enemy through tradition has defiled many altars. You can have a pure heart but be operating in tradition, and the enemy has legal ground to stop the covenant blessing. He is a legalist accomplishing his goal through deception.

If the windows of heaven are not open to you, and you tithe, ask the Lord to show you any areas of impurity personally or corporately, and pray them out!

Chapter 3
Covenant-Destroying Tradition

The second major tradition causing impurity at the altar comes from the traditional way we teach tithing. We teach Malachi 3:8-10 as a *distribution* passage, when it really is a *purpose* passage.

> **Bring all the tithes into the storehouse,**
>
> **That there may be meat in My house.**

We, by tradition, have emphasized "Bring all the tithes into the storehouse" because it suits our purpose without honoring the obligation to fulfill "That there may be meat in My house." We have preached, "Bring the tithe here," while glossing over the real intent of this scripture.

God is quite specific about whom He gave the tithe to! Misleading God's people brings impurity to the altar; especially when done with a motivation for self-gain. Numbers 18 is one of the distribution passages, and verses 19 through 22 show clearly God's intent for the tithe:

> **All the heave offerings of the holy things, which the children of Israel offer to the Lord, *I have given to* you and your sons and daughters with you as an ordinance forever; it is a covenant of salt forever before the Lord with you and your descendants with you.**

> **The Lord said to Aaron: "You shall have no inheritance in their land, nor shall you have any portion among them; I am your portion and your inheritance among the children of Israel.**

"Behold, I have given the *children of Levi all* the tithes in Israel as an inheritance in return for the work which they perform, the work of the tabernacle of meeting.

"Hereafter the children of Israel shall not come near the tabernacle of meeting, lest they bear sin and die."

The scripture does not say God gave the tithe to the local synagogue, as we have traditionally preached. He gave it to the Levites and immediately added, "You had better not assume a Levitical position, lest you die."

God certainly knows human nature as it relates to money! He knows the heart of man, and acts accordingly. God gave the tithe to the Levites and admonished the people not to assume a Levitical position for financial reasons.

As long as we preach that the tithe belongs to the storehouse, those who are not called will start them.

False Pastors

The fruit of our tradition is, in some cases, people who are neither gifted nor called to fivefold positions establishing churches for the wrong reason. The traditional understanding of the tithe entices individuals to step out of their God-ordained gifting and calling to "pastor" individually.

We have, in the Church world today, quite a variety of one-man shows pastoring who are, in fact, gifted and called to other areas. Some feel compelled to do so in order to obtain a paycheck and support their families. In effect, through tradition, we have institutionalized a traditional understanding of the tithe and in the process destroyed the very covenant foundation for God's intended blessing in our lives.

God *did* say to bring the tithe into the storehouse, but when does a ministry qualify as a Bible storehouse, and when does it not? We assume just because a sign out front says XYZ Church, Services Sunday 10 a.m. and 6 p.m., it is a storehouse. Nothing could be further from the truth!

Nowhere in the New Testament is *one* man pointed to as

the "pastor," but shepherding was a recognized function of the elders called and gifted by God in at least five major areas.

The Bible guarantees judgment and removal when people assume positions because of wrong motivation. God always gives a season of grace in which to discern, repent, and obey.

Numbers 18:23,24 says:

> **But the Levites shall perform the work of the tabernacle of meeting, and they shall bear their iniquity; it shall be a statue forever, throughout your generations, that among the children of Israel they shall have no inheritance.**
>
> **For the tithes of the children of Israel, which they offer up as a heave offering to the Lord, I have given to the Levites....**

What was the purpose of giving the tithe to the Levites? In Malachi 3, it was "That there may be meat in My house." Second Chronicles 31:4,5 is very distinctive in its application, as it fully corroborates Malachi 3 in decreeing the purpose for the tithe:

> **Moreover he commanded the people who dwelt in Jerusalem to contribute support for the priests and the Levites, that they might *devote themselves to the Law of the Lord.***
>
> **As soon as the commandment was circulated, the children of Israel brought in abundance the firstfruits of grain and wine, oil and honey, and of all the produce of the field; and they brought in abundantly the *tithe* of everything.**

The scripture is clear and consistent. In Numbers 18, Second Chronicles 31, and Malachi 3, the stated purpose of the tithe is to support the Levites, plural not singular. It was given to the Levites, through the storehouse, so they might devote themselves to the word of the Lord and bring the meat of the word to God's people, causing growth and maturity. But who are the Levites?

The answer to that question lies in understanding types and shadows of the three priesthoods in the Old Testament. From highest to lowest they are: Melchizedek, Aaron, and

Levites. Melchizedek was a type and a shadow of the Lord Jesus Christ, according to Hebrews 7.

Hebrews 7:4-11 says:

Now consider how great this man was [Melchizedek], to whom even the patriarch Abraham gave a tenth of the spoils.

And indeed those who are of the sons of Levi, who receive the priesthood, have a commandment to receive tithes from the people according to the law, that is, from their brethren, though they have come from the loins of Abraham;

but he [Melchizedek] whose genealogy is not derived from them received tithes from Abraham and blessed him who had the promises.

Abraham, in obedience to God, instituted the tithe long before the law ever came into being. The covenant of the tithe transcends the law and is still in force today!

Now beyond all contradiction the lesser is blessed by the better.

Here mortal men receive tithes, *but there he receives them,* of whom it is witnessed that *he [Jesus] lives.*

Even Levi, who receives tithes, paid tithes through Abraham, so to speak,

for he was still in the loins of his father when Melchizedek met him.

Therefore, if perfection were through the Levitical priesthood (for under it the people received the law), what further need was there that another priest should rise according to the order of Melchizedek, and *not be called* according to the order of Aaron?

Aaron's high priesthood was, in many ways, a type and a shadow of Jesus' ministry, but in one major way was not, while Melchizedek's was, according to Hebrews 7. Aaron's priesthood was temporal; it would end at his death and must be passed to another. Melchizedek, without father or mother, was a type of the eternal Priest Jesus, whose ministry will never pass away! In some ways, Aaron has done double duty, because he represents (as a type and a shadow) aspects of both Christ's ministry and the New Testament believer's. Consequently, Jesus is called "...the first-born among many brethren."

In what way did God consider all His saints in the New Covenant and say, "You have an Aaronic ministry?" What did Aaron do that was prophetic of the believer? He personally went into the Holy of Holies once a year.

Matthew 27:51 records at the death of Jesus, the veil of the Temple was torn in two, from top to bottom, as a sign the price had been paid for all to come before the Father. Suddenly, for the first time, the way was open for all the people to come before the Lord. Hebrews 9:8 puts it this way:

> ...the Holy Spirit indicating this, that the way into the Holiest of All was not yet made manifest while the first tabernacle was still standing.

What only Aaron, the High Priest, could do once a year in coming into God's presence in Old Testament times has now been made possible for all New Testament believers to do daily.

The Levitical Ministry

We can go into the presence of God, offer sacrifices of praise, and make intercession for sinners according to God's perfect will and plan. In many ways, Aaron is a type and a shadow of the New Testament believer, but who, then, are the Levites (the third and lowest form of priesthood in the Old Testament)?

Numbers 8:13-19 gives valuable insight into the Levitical ministry:

> And you shall stand the Levites before Aaron and his sons, and then offer them as though a wave offering to the Lord.
>
> Thus you shall separate the Levites from among the children of Israel, and the Levites shall be Mine.
>
> After that the Levites shall go in to service the tabernacle

of meeting. So you shall cleanse them and offer them, as though a wave offering.

For they are wholly given to Me from among the children of Israel; I have taken them for Myself instead of all who open the womb, the firstborn of all the children of Israel.

For all the firstborn among the children of Israel are Mine, both man and beast; on the day that I struck all the firstborn in the land of Egypt I sanctified them to Myself.

I have taken the Levites instead of all the firstborn of the children of Israel.

I have given the Levites as a gift to Aaron and his sons from among the children of Israel, to do the work for the children of Israel in the tabernacle of meeting, and to make atonement for the children of Israel....

Three corresponding scriptures have "thats" which fit together, contributing to our accurately understanding the tithe. Malachi 3:10 says:

Bring the tithes into the storehouse *that*, there may be meat in My house."

Second Chronicles 31:4 says:

...*that* the Levites may devote themselves to the word of the Lord

Numbers 8:19 says:

...*that* there be no plague among the children of Israel when the children of Israel come near....

The Levites were to mature the believers by teaching God's Word. They were to make people aware of God's requirements so that no plague fell upon the people when coming near God. The Levites were charged with preparing people to fulfill covenant purposes through understanding God's Word.

Who are the New Testament Levites? Verse 19 says they were given as *"gifts to Aaron."* Ephesians 4:7-11 also speaks of gifts given to New Testament Aarons.

But to each one of us grace was given according to the measure of Christ's gift.

Therefore He says: "When He ascended on high, He led captivity captive, And gave gifts to men."

(Now this, "He ascended" — what does it mean but that He also descended into the lower parts of the earth?

He who descended is also the One who ascended far above all the heavens, that He might fill all things.)

And He Himself gave some to be *apostles*, some *prophets*, some *evangelists*, and some *pastors*, and *teachers*....

Who are the New Testament Levites? Apostles, prophets, evangelists, pastors, and teachers. Is the purpose of this New Testament Levitical ministry the same as that of the Old Testament Levites?

Verse 12:

for the equipping of the saints for the working of ministry, for the edifying of the body of Christ,

till we all come to the unity of the faith and the knowledge of the Son of God, to a perfect (or mature) man, to the measure of the stature of the fullness of Christ;

that we should no longer be children, tossed to and fro and carried about with every wind of doctrine, by the trickery of men, in the cunning craftiness by which they lie in wait to deceive....

It appears the same purpose is stated here, but in slightly different language. They are both called *gifts*. They both have the purpose of maturing the saints by bringing forth meat. Both contribute to helping people walk in a way pleasing to God through the fullness of His covenant, where there will be no plague or deception among God's people. The purpose is basically the same!

When preaching the tithe, we said, "If you tithe, God will open the windows of heaven to you." This left people with a half-truth.

About eight years ago, I was going home from what in all outward appearances was a great meeting. The anointing was strong on the teaching, and God moved in various gifts of the Spirit, but I could not shake inner dissatisfaction. By all the standard criteria, it was a dynamite meeting, but in my spirit there was something missing.

As I asked the Lord what was wrong, the Holy Spirit said, "Son, it is not what you told them that is the problem. What was said was true and good. It is what you did *not* tell them that will get them in trouble."

At that point, I realized it was not enough to bring forth a measure of truth in a service. There is a tendency at times when you have a teaching ministry to want to unload everything you know about a subject all at once. You can't do it in most cases because of time limitations.

A New Accountability

God was calling me to a new accountability in measuring out the truth and bringing it forth fully balanced so people would not run with part of the answer and end up in misapplication. God holds us responsible. James 3 says the teaching ministry has the greatest accountability of all.

In Matthew 23:16-19, as Jesus deals with hypocrisy, He confronts the Scribes and Pharisees and rebukes the entire religious system:

> Woe to you, blind guides, who say, "Whoever swears by the temple, it is nothing; but whoever swears by the gold of the temple, he is obliged to perform it."
>
> Fools and blind! For which is greater, the gold or the temple that sanctifies the gold?
>
> And,"whoever swears by the altar, it is nothing; but whoever swears by the gift that is on it, he is obliged to perform it."
>
> Fools and blind! For which is greater, the gift or the altar that sanctifies the gift?

We did in our preaching what we learned in Bible school and made the gift more important than the altar. It is not what we told people that got them in trouble, but what we did *not* tell them. We did not tell them because we did not know how to discern impure altars.

Jesus made one thing clear: It is not your tithe and offering in itself which makes the covenant work. What makes the covenant work is the union of God's purpose, an individual's obedient heart with purity in the altar where they give their tithe. Purity completes the covenant and guarantees fulfilled promises.

The condition of the altar either makes the tithe holy or unholy, pure or impure, accepted or rejected.

When you put tithe or offering on an impure altar, you lose your covenant promise for God's multiplication and increase. God is not obligated, because the money is not sanctified.

A perfect example of how the enemy has attacked the Church is seen in Joshua 6, where Israel was beginning to possess the Promised Land. They could not talk or say a word for seven long days. God was teaching them obedience!

"The Tithe Is Mine"

Jericho was the only city where God said, "You cannot have any of the spoil. It all belongs to Me." Jericho became a type of the tithe, or first ten percent. In every other city, God said, "The spoil is yours." But in the very first city He said, "It is mine. Do not touch it." The two Hebrew words used to describe the spoil of Jericho are *kheh-rem* and *khaw-ram*.

In the Lexical Aids to the Old Testament section of *The Hebrew Greek Key Study Bible*, *kheh-rem* is described as follows:

> It was an object. The essential meaning is "forbidden" or "prohibited" which was surrendered to God into His service or something declared for utter destruction. The most famous example was the entire city of Jericho and everything in it (Joshua 6:17).

> Everything flammable was to be burned or reserved for God. However, Achan took some things which were in the city. This caused the whole nation of Israel to be affected by the violation.

> They lost an easy battle at Ai (Joshua 7:12,13). Sin was in the camp and it had to be removed before God would make them victorious again. Jericho was a pagan city which defi-

antly opposed God's work. *Through Achan, Israel unwittingly became associated with Jericho.*

The Hebrew root word for *kheh-rem* is *khaw-ram*. Lexical Aids to the Old Testament says, "The basic idea was that of setting something aside strictly for God's use. It was considered most holy by God, and therefore could not be sold or redeemed by any substitutionary measure."

It is clear from studying these words that they carry two basic ideas: (1) they described items to be surrendered or given over to God, and (2) they implied both the blessing for obedience and a curse for disobedience, which is also part of the covenant language used in Malachi 3.

Interestingly enough, the same two Hebrew words are used to describe the tithe as "devoted or holy" to the Lord in Leviticus 27:28-30:

> **Nevertheless no devoted [kheh-rem] offering that a man may devote [kheh-rem] to the Lord of all that he has, both man and beast, or the field of his possession, shall be sold or redeemed; every devoted [kheh-rem] offering is most holy to the Lord.**

> **No person [kheh-rem] under the ban, who may become doomed [khaw-ram] to destruction among men, shall be redeemed, but shall surely be put to death.**

> **And all the tithe of the land, whether of the seed of the land or of the fruit of the tree, is the Lord's. It is holy to the Lord.**

Studying this Hebrew word in Joshua opens our understanding to see the impact our tradition is having on the financial condition of the Body of Christ.

We find the word *kheh-rem* in Joshua 7:1:

> **But the children of Israel committed a trespass regarding the accursed [kheh-rem] things, Achan the son of Carmi, the son of Zabdi, the son of Zerah, of the tribe of Judah took of the accursed [kheh-rem] things; so the anger of the Lord burned against the children of Israel.**

Achan took for himself what had been dedicated to God!

Joshua was fresh from a great victory at Jericho. He sent spies to Ai. The spies returned, saying, "Do not send everyone there. It is a small place. It is a waste for all the children of Israel to go up. Just send a few people up there and we will take it." Joshua sent three thousand men. They should have taken it, but they could not. They were beaten, and they did not know why.

Joshua fell on his face, crying, "God, why did You ever bring us over the Jordan?" As if to say, "God, it is your fault." God said, "Why are you crying and blubbering before Me, Joshua? Get up. There is a reason: The covenant has been transgressed." It is not working!

Israel has sinned, and they have also transgressed My covenant which I commanded them. For they have even taken some of the accursed *[kheh-rem]* things, and have both stolen and deceived; and they have also put it among their own stuff.

Therefore the children of Israel *could not stand* before their enemies, but turned their backs before their enemies, because they have become doomed to destruction.

Tithing Today

What does this account have to do with tithing today? God gave the tithe to the Levites. The five New Testament ministries of Ephesians 4 are among those who obviously qualify as modern-day Levites. They are apostles, prophets, evangelists, pastors, teachers.

When any one of these five claims for himself the whole tithe, he is doing spiritually exactly what Achan did physically — with the same impact on God's army. God said, "You are doomed to destruction. You cannot stand before your enemies." Studying this, I suddenly saw the full magnitude of what the devil has done through tradition.

In the majority of our churches every Sunday we say or imply, "It is time to bring the tithes and offerings into the storehouse." Many a message has been preached on the fact the storehouse is the local church, but we neglected the full truth.

Nowhere in scripture did God ever say He gave the tithe to the local synagogue. He said He gave it to the Levites. When any one of the New Testament Levitical ministries individually claims all the tithe without having a commitment to all five functional and operational, he is doing to his people exactly what Achan did to Israel.

How many times has the local church been portrayed as the full storehouse, when it was at best only a partial one? When one man thinks he can do it all without any consideration for the remainder of the Levitical ministry, impurity reigns.

God never intended that one gifting should bring a congregation of people to maturity. That concept is found nowhere in the New Testament. In fact, what is set before us as normal church structure is exactly the opposite! It takes input from all five gifts to bring anybody into the full measure of the stature of Jesus Christ.

The Theological Word Book of the New Testament, or "Kittels," generally considered the definitive work in New Testament Greek, says in Volume 2, page 617, concerning the Greek word *ep-is-kop-os*:

> There is no reference to monarchical episcopate. [That means one-man traditional pastoral rule.] On the contrary, the evidence of the New Testament is clearly to the effect that originally several episcopi took charge of the communities in brotherly comity.

Kittel also indicates that in the Early Church, the only time pastors were in the pulpit was when the apostle, prophet, and teacher were out of town! In Volume 2, page 617, after discussing the characteristics of the *ep-is-kop-os*, which is the Greek word usually translated "bishop," he says:

> There is a parallel passage in Titus 1:5-9. Titus had the task of appointing elders in the cities of Crete as Paul had done in Asia Minor according to Acts 14:23. This was the way to ensure the continued life of the churches once the missionaries had gone.

The qualifications of presbyters here are like those of the bishops [ep-is-kop-os] in 1 Timothy 3:2 ff. In fact, there is an alternation of terms in Titus1:7, where we suddenly have ep-is-kop-os instead of presbuteros. This is another proof that the two terms originally referred to the same thing, namely, the guidance and representation of the congregation and the work of preaching and conducting worship when there was no apostle, prophet or teacher present.

The picture Kittel presents is quite different from what we have inherited by tradition. By any one of the five ministry gifts claiming the tithe based on Malachi 3, ("Bring all the tithes into the storehouse...") and disregarding Biblical purpose for the tithe, which was for all Levites, we have corrupted the covenant and defiled the altar.

12 Corrupting Influences

By misusing Malachi 3:10, we have opened the door to twelve corrupting influences currently plaguing believers!

The twelve fruits of teaching the tithe as a formula are:

1. People become equated with money. Thus, the more people you get, the larger your budget.

2. Success in ministry is judged by numbers in the congregation, or on your mailing list, rather than fulfillment of the divine call.

3. Church growth becomes paramount and church growth seminars are popular, but often for the wrong motivation.

4. Competition for the saints among leadership grows because more people translate into more money.

5. Envy and jealousy rise among leadership over the size of their ministries.

6. Rich businessmen are recruited for special board positions, violating James 2 and the true purpose of deacons. (For a fuller understanding of this defilement, see the tape series "Getting God's Heart, 'The Real Deacons'")

7. There is a growing pressure to refuse to preach any-

thing controversial or offensive because it might dry up our funding.

8. Ministries are tempted to use Madison Avenue marketing techniques to woo people and build the mailing list, rather than praying for old-fashioned revival.

9. The saints are hindered in developing a confidence in hearing the Lord's voice through giving because they only relate to Him by formula.

10. Believers are strengthened in an unscriptural attitude of "works righteousness" by fulfilling a formula rather than learning to relate personally.

11. Many people are progressively overcome by discouragement because the promise of blessing and open windows never comes in the measure God promises.

12. Fiercely sectarian doctrine arises, erecting barriers which keep the saints in "our" camp (the motivation is often financial), causing divisions and barriers hindering the unity of the faith which God has ordained.

Spiritual Politicians

Only the Lord knows how many organizations have been infiltrated by spiritual politicians who long to climb the ladder of success in position, power, influence, and prosperity, thereby defiling the altar rather than embracing the Biblical motivation of service. The fruit of our inherited tradition is, in many places apparent: Division, disharmony, disunity, and strife prevail.

In spite of our current state, I believe God has ordained the Church to be the center of spiritual activity in these end-times. It is the place where spiritual "spot-remover" is applied, wrinkles are ironed out, and blemishes excised! I believe the Church has been ordained of God to become the center of all activity where the supervision, training, and release of an end-time army brings in the greatest harvest the earth has ever produced.

During the decade of the '70s, there was a move of the

Holy Spirit which seemed to be centered not in the churches, but in convention centers instead! The pastors of that era made the convention center ministries because they would not allow them in their pulpits.

Each of the fivefold ministries has a distinct and unique shepherding function, according to Acts 20 and First Peter 5, yet what distinguishes the shepherd from the shepherding function of the other four is the heart which he or she has for the people.

The Hireling Mentality

The difference between a true shepherd and a hireling is not difficult to spot (Mark 6:30-42). *The hireling is generally afraid to have other ministries of equal status around which he cannot control.* He wants everybody to know he is the undisputed, number one leader. Everybody else submits to him. He is everyone else's covering! Who is his covering? He submits to no man except to the Lord.

The hireling is generally afraid to have other ministries around, because they are a threat to his position. He jealously guards position above everything else.

The true shepherd, on the other hand, looks to his flock. He wants to make sure each of them is fed, and he realizes he usually has only one of the five ingredients necessary to bring them to a place of maturity and satisfaction in the Lord [1]. The true shepherd actually demands other ministries come in and bring his people the balanced diet they so desperately need!

In Mark 6:30-42 the twelve were tired. They wanted to rest. They hadn't even had time to eat. Jesus demonstrates the heart of the true shepherd! He made them stay until the people's needs were met, recognizing one man could not serve by himself.

I believe the days of the one-man show are over. In days gone by, many congregations only had one man, because that is all they could support. But as God restores ministry to the Biblical pattern, He will raise up individuals who can and will gladly, willingly, go into churches, not requiring anything financially, even as Paul did, because they know God is involved in their ministry and will meet the need.

The true heart of the traveling ministry does not require a specified amount that unfairly burdens the local congregation. Neither does it leave unpaid bills behind when it leaves town. The pure heart of a traveling ministry is to build up the local body and to deposit in the people what they recognize God has first put in them, believing and expecting that one place's abundance will take care of another place's lack.

---

[1] For a more complete understanding of each gift and multiple-gifting, see the tape series "After God's Own Heart."

Chapter 4
Manipulation, A Major Root of Impurity

If tradition is the number one source of impurity at the altar, it is only ahead of manipulation by a hair! Manipulation, like tradition, can be a part of your life as standard operating procedure and you do not even realize it!

In December 1984, the Lord spoke these words to me: "No longer sell your books and tapes, but make them available on a 'pray and obey' basis."

My experience had conditioned me to believe that between 15 and 30 percent of the monthly budget for traveling ministries came directly from the tape and book table.

At that particular time, my ministry desperately needed a new car, walk-around microphone, and a variety of additional equipment totaling several thousand dollars. The money was just not available for any of it.

Nevertheless, I made the commitment to no longer sell books and tapes for one year. Looking up to heaven, with finger pointed at God, I said, "Lord, I am going to do this for one year, and if You do not honor it, that's all!"

So my initial commitment to "pray and obey" was for one year — the year 1985. The second week of January, I was doing a seminar in a church in San Diego that had about five hundred people. The first night I explained the "pray and obey" system, saying we no longer sold books and tapes. I walked back to the tape tables after the service, and we were swamped with what appeared to be two-legged vacuum cleaners!

I went back to the motel room that night and totaled up the cost to put everything on the table that had walked out the door. The total was $999.64 in actual cost, or $2500 at retail value. In the "pray and obey" basket that night was $58. I looked up to heaven, pointed my finger at the Lord, and said, "This was *your* idea, and it is not working!"

Every week for the next three months, as I would get the ministry's weekly financial summary from my secretary, I was in utter amazement. It was as if God opened the windows of heaven for a season, and after three months, I was believing God again!

God's Way Works

The Lord honored that commitment. We were not only able to buy a car for our ministry, but one of equal value for a missionary, plus all the other equipment we needed. The Lord proved to me that He would supply the need of the ministry if I would but obey!

The thing that changed my life was what God said to me the night I returned from the first "pray and obey" meeting with only $58. I told the Lord, "This was your idea, not mine, and it is not working." God's response to my prayer assault was Second Chronicles 16:9. It was a verse I was familiar with in part. The part I recognized was:

For the eyes of the Lord run to and fro throughout the whole earth, looking for those whose heart is perfect toward Him, that He may show Himself strong in their behalf.

I said, "Lord, what does it mean to have a perfect heart?" He said, "Go back to the beginning." The account deals with King Asa. To go back to the beginning, you have to return to Second Chronicles 14-16. These chapters portray the life of Asa before the Lord and what happened to him as a result of his choices.

Asa started out his ministry walking hand in hand with the Lord. "He removed the altars of the foreign gods in the high places, broke down the sacred pillars, and cut down the wooden images. He commanded Judah to seek the Lord God of their fathers and observe the law and the commandments."

Asa was unafraid to go to war. The Ethiopians came out against him with a million men and three hundred chariots, but because Asa readily acknowledged his utter dependence on God and was willing to go to war, God came through on his behalf. Asa was victorious over the Ethiopians, even though outnumbered two to one! Then came a warning:

> **The Lord is with you while you are with Him. If you seek Him, He will be found by you; but if you forsake Him, He will forsake you.**

> **2 Chronicles 15:2**

There had been a famine of the teaching of God's Word in the land, and the prophecy came forth that restoration was the intent and plan for that season. Asa responded. Everyone followed his leadership and entered into a covenant to seek the Lord God with all their heart and with all their soul. The result was, God gave them twenty years of peace and blessing.

After these two decades of peace and prosperity, the enemy once again attacked Judah. They cut off all the trade. Rather than going out to war, as he had done earlier, wholly trusting in God, Asa took the silver and gold from the treasuries of the house of the Lord and used them for another purpose!

He hired Ben-Hadad, king of Syria, who had always been an enemy of Judah, to go attack Baasha, king of Israel. This was common practice in the world of that day and it worked. King Asa got what he wanted, but he did not do it God's way. The Lord sent Hanani the prophet to rebuke Asa. His words are recorded in the second part of verse 9, which I had somehow missed:

> **...In this you have done foolishly; therefore from now on you shall have wars.**

What Asa did was use *manipulation* to get what he wanted. Interestingly enough, it worked. But the price he paid to get what he wanted man's way was tremendous! Asa forfeited victories God would have given him, and from that point on he would have wars, because he was not willing to do what needed to be done God's way.

Spiritual law dictates whenever a ministry begins to use manipulation, rather than trusting God financially, it will work for a season. The fruit of manipulation in the long term is continual financial wars. *Manipulation destroys your ability to walk with God!* Verses 12 and 13 of chapter 16 say:

And in the thirty-nineth year of his reign, Asa became diseased in his feet, and his malady was very severe; yet in his disease he did not seek the Lord, but the physicians.

So Asa rested with his fathers; he died in the forty-first year of his reign.

Asa came to the place where he could no longer trust God for healing, and he had to go to the physicians. There is nothing wrong with going to doctors. That is not what this scripture is teaching.

The Spirit of Manipulation

What it teaches us is that the spirit of manipulation can gain such a foothold in your life you no longer have a foundation on which to approach God in faith. It seems so easy to get what you want through manipulation, you lose your ability to trust God for it.

It is especially a warning to those of us who live in the last days when the spirit of manipulation will, in fact, become a very important part of the counterfeit trinity deceptively duplicating the move of the Holy Spirit.

Examples of financial manipulation are more and more obvious, following the natural progression until destruction falls. One fund-raiser I saw recently quoted scriptures out of the Book of Acts:

And God wrought special miracles by the hands of Paul: So that from his body were brought unto the sick handkerchiefs or aprons, and the diseases departed from them, and the evil spirits went out of them.

When you get a full-page color ad in the mail saying, "God told me to loan you a piece of my handkerchief," with an urgent return envelope, you should be suspicious! Examples of what can be done with the special handkerchief were given. You could lay it on a person for their healing, lay it on your old car for another one, lay it on your wallet for money to meet a budget or pay bills, lay it on your house for another one, and as you follow the steps that carefully tell you what to do, of course the last one says, "Return the handkerchief or prayer request and the best gift you can come up with."

There is a major difference between what happened in Acts 19 and what is advertised in some cases today. The difference is Paul never sent his handkerchief with a return envelope telling people to immediately send back their best love gift! Paul's motivation was pure. I am not so sure about some of those I see today.

If you lay that fund-raising handkerchief on yourself, you are likely to get a double dose of what's driving the sender instead of Bible promises! It is very possible something can be transferred that you really do not want.

Classes in Fund-Raising

Manipulation is being developed to a fine art. You can take classes in fund-raising and learn how to write appeal letters, or easier yet, buy a package of "proven performers" guaranteed to extract every available penny from every widow on your mailing list!

One of the quickest ways to defile an altar is to bring in professional fund-raisers, who are generally paid a percentage of what they raise, which makes it quite obvious what their motivation is in everything they do. Any project that requires a professional fund-raiser to bring it to pass, was not originated by God to start with!

Like anything else Satan offers, once you start using manipulation, more is required each time to produce the same results. The pathway to addiction is the same for ministry business practices as it is for drugs.

The whole Church can agree deliverance is needed for drug addicts, but can we see the same deliverance is needed for some of our ministry business conduct because its roots are in the same devil.

Mailing lists are bought and sold frequently in Christian circles today. That in itself is a violation of integrity. If you have ever received mail you didn't request, your name and address was probably sold for a fee! We need a Holy Ghost vaccination against the disastrous deadly disease of manipulation.

We have a mailing list for a daily Bible study, entitled the"Word at Work." We refuse to put people on it unsolicited. When one person requests we send it to a friend, we enclose a note saying, "We are sending you this material compliments of *your friend.* If you would like to continue receiving it, please return the enclosed card." Their name only goes on the list if they choose to continue receiving it! This is simple, basic, foundational ministerial integrity.

We have an obligation to teach believers how to discern the true from the false. If you are in a meeting and the big push for money comes forth — do you really think it is a manifestation of the Holy Spirit?

You will usually hear, "The Lord has impressed me that ten people are going to give $1,000, or twenty-five people will give $500" or, depending on the size of the meeting, "One hundred people will give $100, or five hundred will give $50."

When To Walk Out

If God really said that, what is the need for people to publicly stand and acknowledge the call, violating Jesus' admonition to give in secret? This kind of fund-raising bears the marks of flesh, not spirit! If you are in a meeting and hear the words, "I'm not going to preach unless we get $50,000,"or whatever amount, do yourself a favor — get up and walk out!

What God wants to do, He can pay for without man's help!

Even the Christian publishing world seems inundated with profiteers. When a new author first has a best-selling work, the publisher usually comes back immediately and pressures him for a second book. The publisher's motivation for a second work is usually financial. That defiles the work before it is ever written. Anyone who preaches or publishes what God gives for profit deserves to have some of the proceeds spent paying the personal expenses of an early departure.

On two occasions in Jesus' earthly ministry, He "cleaned house" in the Temple. As we look at our Church world today, it is obvious we are due for another one.

I do not believe there is anything wrong with selling books or tapes. What defiles an altar is the *motivation* for advertising, production, and distribution. When you see a man in the pulpit taking an inordinate amount of time advertising his books and tapes, he usually is being pressured to meet his budget, and without knowing it has brought impurity to his altar.

When I told the Lord "pray and obey" was His idea and it was not working, He gave me Second Chronicles 16:9 and said, "I finally got you in a place where I can bless you." I did not understand that. I had to pray and seek God for the interpretation.

Prior to January 1985, when I would go into churches where I knew my budget would probably not be met, sometimes I would take a few minutes to talk about books and tapes, because anytime you mention them, people will go back to the tables and ask for them. When I did this occasionally, I did not even realize what I was doing. You can do things in ministry because of pressure that your mind will justify.

What God was saying to me was, "Now that I have purified your altar by removing manipulation, I can begin to bless it." I believe the right attitude appears in the life of the Apostle Paul:

Did I commit sin in abasing myself that you might be exalted, because I preached the gospel of God to you *free of charge?*

I robbed other churches, taking wages from them to minister to you.

And when I was present with you, and in need, I was a burden to no one, for what was lacking to me the brethren who came from Macedonia supplied. And in everything *I kept myself from being burdensome* to you, and so I will keep myself.

As the truth of Christ is in me, no one shall stop me this boasting in the regions of Achaia.

Why? Because I do not love you? God knows!

2 Corinthians 11:7-11

Motives for Publishing

Paul kept himself from being a burden to the churches. Today we make ourselves a burden! Paul was emphatic on one point: "There is one thing I live by. I preach the Gospel of Christ to you *free of charge.*" I believe a principle that separates ministries is, "To what degree are we committed to this truth?"

How many Christian books would be written if they had to be made available to people by grace and could not be sold? That in itself would put the brakes on all projects being published for the wrong motivation. I am not recommending everyone immediately quit selling books and tapes, but ask yourself, as a check on your own heart, "Would I continue to do this if I could not expect any profit from it?"

Every man or woman of God called to full-time ministry must come to grips with Second Corinthians 2:17 (*NIV*):

Unlike so many, we do not peddle the word for profit. On the contrary, in Christ we speak before God with sincerity, *like men sent from God*

The Greek word translated "peddle", is *kap-ale-yoo-o,* with the following meanings, according to the *Hebrew-Greek Key Study Bible,* "To treat as if for personal profit, profiteer, to

44

adulterate the wine; to make a gain of anything. A huckster or petty retail trader. Adulterating not simply for the sake of it, but making an unworthy personal gain thereby. Profiteering from God's Word, preaching for money or professing faith for personal gain."

The Amplified Bible says,

> **For we are not, like so many (as hucksters, tavern keepers, making a trade of) peddling God's Word — short measuring and adulterating the divine message....**

When you have to spend five or ten minutes advertising, promoting, and selling records, books, or tapes just to stay on television or radio, God probably didn't tell you to go on the air to start with!

What God tells a man to do, He pays for without manipulation. How will we ever qualify for the next mighty move of the Spirit using such worldly tactics?

Peter demonstrates the mind-set we need to have in Acts 3:6, when he says,

> **Silver and gold I do not have, but what *I do have* I give you: In the name of Jesus Christ of Nazareth, rise up and walk.**

In Acts 5, all who came for healing received. Do we *have* what Peter had? If not, why not?

Why could God trust Peter with that kind of authority but not trust our generation? The reason should be obvious! If there ever was a man who could easily profit from an anointing, it was Peter. People were healed when his shadow passed over them. Acts 5:16 records every person who came was delivered and healed. Peter refused to advertise, sell, and promote in order to personally profit from his anointing! His personal intergrity opened the door to divine authority. Peter's attitude toward peddling is clearly revealed in his dealings with a new convert named Simon.

Before conversion, Simon was a magician making money through the magical arts. A common practice was to buy secrets from the great masters of the day, recouping your money from the people of your own city. Simon had apparently been successful because many called him "...the great power of God (Acts 8:10)."

The *Weymouth* translation has excellent footnotes for the key words in Acts 8:18-23.

> **When, however, Simon saw that it was through the laying on of the Apostles' hands that the Spirit was bestowed, he offered them money.**
>
> **"Give me too," he said, "that power, so every one on whom I place my hands will receive the Holy Spirit."**
>
> **"Perish your money and yourself," replied Peter, "because you have imagined that you can obtain God's free gift with money!**
>
> **"No part or lot have you in this matter, for your heart is not right in God's sight.**
>
> **"Repent, therefore, of this wickedness of yours, and pray to the Lord, in the hope that the purpose which in your heart may perhaps be forgiven you.**
>
> **"For I perceive that you have fallen into the bitterest bondage of unrighteousness."**

Peter was shocked and appalled that anyone would desire God's power for personal gain! Weymouth's footnote on the word "purpose" in verse 22 says, "The purpose was no doubt that of making money out of the spiritual gift."

The most sobering thing of all in this passage is how Peter viewed the spiritual condition of a man who would profiteer from God's giftings. Peter told Simon to repent, "in the hope that" he could be forgiven. Weymouth's footnote on the Greek says, "Lit. 'if (or, whether) therefore.' The exact sense seems to be, 'Find out by prayer *whether*, the offense being so *rank* and therefore the possibility of pardon so *doubtful*, the sin can nevertheless be forgiven.'"

Peter gave a powerful glimpse into God's heart concerning selling the Gospel. The offense is so rank as to make forgiveness doubtful!

Could the Holy Spirit have been any clearer? Are we going to be ministers "sent from God," or powerless petty peddlers?

If the Lord told me to start selling books and tapes again, I would do so without hesitation. The real issue is right motivation of heart. If God is not in it, you had better not publish it! Paul made the Gospel available to people freely, believing God would pay for what He ordained. Can we make the personal commitment Peter and Paul made? Can we rise to that same level of faith?

Paul continues with this theme in Second Corinthians 11:12,13:

> But what I do, I will also continue to do, that I may cut off the opportunity from those who desire an opportunity to be regarded just as we are in the things of which they boast.
>
> For such are false apostles, deceitful workers, transforming themselves into the apostles of Christ.

True Apostles and Prophets

Pastors with pure hearts do not have to be afraid of the *true* emerging apostolic and prophetic ministries. This passage lays down a guideline to judge between the true and the false.

If someone comes saying, "I am an apostle," and demands you hand over authority in your church to him, or says he is a prophet, and demands that you listen and act on his prophetic word without exhibiting the *service motivation*, he is generally a nut, flake, and all-around fruitcake!

The true emerging apostolic and prophetic ministries show the attitude of a servant. Some apostolic ministries are recruiting churches, asking them to give ten percent of what comes in to their local churches according to Numbers 18 as God directed the Levites to support Aaron.

In the first place, Aaron is not, in most respects, a type of fivefold ministry. Aaron was a High Priest for the people.

There is only one High Priest in Christianity; His Name is Jesus. When Hebrews 7 says, "...his priesthood is not after the order of Aaron," it refers to the fact that Aaron died and his ministry ended. But Jesus is alive and His ministry never ends! Many of the things assigned Aaron were direct types of what Jesus would do for us. The fivefold ministry could never do what Jesus did.

To recruit churches at ten percent a month violates the very apostolic principle laid down by the Apostle Paul! He said in Second Corinthians 11:12 and 13, "I will continue to do what I do that I may cut off the opportunity from those who desire an opportunity to be regarded as true apostles."

Paul said the difference between the true and false is obvious. The true do not require a set amount of money, demand quality amenities, have to promote, advertise or market their works. The true can preach and publish without requirements, because they know God is involved in what they are doing.

The false, on the other hand, which do not have the right motivation, have no guarantee of God's backing; therefore, they have to charge, promote, require, and demand.

I am not saying everyone who sells is false, or everyone who recruits churches at ten percent per month is a counterfeit. The real issue is motivation of heart. If the motivation for ministry is financial, impurity reigns!

Paul's Pure Standard

The Apostle Paul set a pure standard. This principle in Paul's life is further borne out by looking in the Book of Philippians.

The Apostle Paul visited Philippi during his second missionary journey and founded the church. He came back during his third missionary journey, and finally wrote the letter while he was in prison in Rome. At this point in time, Paul had three full missionary journeys behind him; he had established many churches, but what did he require of those churches he established?

Did he require ten percent of everything that came in every month? Did he require they put the building in his name? What did Paul require of the churches he, himself, founded? Philippians 4:15, written with just a few years remaining in his life, makes a strong statement for the way Paul conducted his relationship with the local church:

Now you Philippians know also that in the beginning of the gospel, when I departed from Macedonia, no church shared with me concerning giving and receiving but you only.

Paul had established other churches, but he did not require any support from them. He truly lived the principle he taught in Second Corinthians 11. It is amazing to look at organizations that violate this principle today. Many denominations require a percentage, or at least the building or property in their name.

Practices such as this should flash at us like a blinking neon sign, revealing true motivations of the hearts of men! When will we see the full covenant promises of God in manifestation? When once again our altars are pure and we can bring an offering to the Lord in righteousness.

Traveling ministries that make decisions about where to go based strictly on financial potential are in great danger of totally missing God. When the majority of pastors pay a price for years serving faithfully small congregations, how in good conscience can those of us who travel refuse to help, based solely on their inability to pay? Are we serving God or man?

Any minister who recruits people for his "board," worship team, or any other position, based on the wealth of the individual, will disqualify himself for participation in the next great move of the Holy Spirit!

We need to ask ourselves about the real heart motivation for the things we do. What is our motivation for full-page ads in leading Christian publications? We can not be promoters and qualify for the power at the same time.

To live the way Paul lived, you have to *know* God is

involved in what you are doing. Today, in contrast, we can print our material in color, package, promote, and profit from it, and God help the people who buy it! To operate the way many of our churches and ministries operate today, God doesn't even have to be involved. *Which standard will you choose?*

As fivefold ministry gifts given to the Body of Christ, our assignment is to build Jesus into people, not build great ministries for ourselves! I believe God will no longer build great churches or ministries, but instead He will build the Body of Christ! *Which standard will you support?*

Chapter 5
The Offering

 In Malachi 3, God said, "You have robbed Me in tithes and offerings," making it quite clear the covenant includes both.

The purpose of the tithe is clearly stated, but what is the purpose of offerings? The first offering ever taken in scripture was received in Exodus 25:1,2,8,9.

Then the Lord spoke to Moses, saying:

"Speak to the children of Israel, that they bring Me an offering. From everyone who gives it willingly with his heart you shall take My offering....

"And let them make Me a sanctuary, that I may dwell among them.

"According to all that I show you, that is, the pattern of the tabernacle and the pattern of all its furnishings, just so you shall make it."

The offering was to build the tabernacle! One general rule consistently emerges: *offerings* in scripture support *buildings*, while *tithes* support *people*.

What usually happens on Sunday morning in a traditional church when a visiting ministry is present? The standard practice in many churches is to receive tithes and offerings for the local assembly first and then, after the guest has ministered, receive a love offering.

Depending on the inclination of the pastor, sometimes there is a five-minute exhortation about the necessity of the tithe given to the church. If all the tithers in Christendom had the testimony "The windows of heaven are open," we would know we are operating correctly. However, when the majority of believers agree God's promises for tithing have not come, something is definitely wrong! Have our traditions made the Word of God of none effect? Does prevailing tradition have us using tithe and offering totally backwards?

If Exodus 25 is not just a one-time event, and God expected people to continually use the offering for the building, we would certainly expect to see, in scripture, other references to offerings used for buildings.

Solomon's Temple, after many years, fell into disrepair. The king in power at the time was named Jehoash. According to Second Chronicles and the corresponding passage in Second Kings, Jehoash, also called Joash, gave the following admonition:

> And Jehoash said to the priests, "All the money of the dedicated gifts that are brought into the house of the Lord — each man's census money, each man's assessment money — and all the money that a man purposes in his heart to bring into the house of the Lord,

> "let the priests take it themselves, each from his constituency; and let them repair the damages of the temple, wherever any dilapidation is found."

Second Kings 12:4,5 becomes quite interesting when interpreted in the light of the corresponding passage in Second Chronicles 24. There can be no doubt that these are offerings taken according to the commandment of Moses, who initiated offerings for the Temple.

God is consistent. In His plan, the Temple, or meeting place, was built and maintained by offerings, while the Levites were supported through tithes. It is so complete and consistent in scripture as to bring us to a place of conviction as to how we use tithe and offering today.

Three specific offerings are referred to: (1) census, (2) assessment, and (3) free will. In Second Chronicles 24:5,6, the leaders were convinced God had ordained offerings to be taken, not tithes, for the preservation and continual upkeep of the building.

> Then he gathered the priests and the Levites, and said to them, "Go out to the cities of Judah, and gather from all Israel money to repair the house of your God from year to year, and see that you do it quickly." However the Levites did not do it quickly.

> So the king called Jehoiada the chief priest, and said to him, "Why have you not required the Levites to bring in from Judah and from Jerusalem the collection, *according to the commandment of Moses* the servant of the Lord and of the congregation of Israel, for the tabernacle of witness?"

God's Plan for Giving

This passage refers us back to Exodus 25, where the very first offering was taken. Using offerings for the building was God's plan then and seems to be now! It has always been God's plan. We have been taught offerings are for other ministries which come in as special guest speakers, or for those outside the local church. What does this produce?

The fruit of this perversion is twofold. First, it contributes to the testimony of the believers, who have done their best to obey what leadership has taught by tithing faithfully, yet they have not seen the promise which was preached to them.

Second, we see good men with excellent ministries pastoring when they could be much more effective in their true calling, but the local church has become the only place they can preach the tithe and pay the bills.

Competition between pastors and leaders of churches, which God never intended, has grown to an all-time high. Jesus clearly said, "A house divided against itself cannot stand," yet the competition from financial pressure is evident in practically every city in North America.

We will never have unity and harmony in leadership without a return to the Biblical standard. The saints have to

be released and taught to obey the leadership of the Holy
Spirit, not man's formula in giving.

When a house of prayer is transformed into a den of
thieves, Jesus will soon appear with broom in hand!

This heading appears in Deuteronomy 12, of *The Open
Bible Study Edition*: "The Law of the Central Sanctuary."
Today we do not have one central sanctuary nationally like
Israel had, but the demand for purity is the same!

**These are the statutes and judgments which you shall be
careful to observe in the land which the Lord God of your
fathers is giving you to possess, all the days that you live on
the earth.**

**You shall utterly destroy all the places where the nations
which you shall dispossess served their gods, on the high
mountains and on the hills and under every green tree.**

**And you shall destroy their altars, break their sacred pil-
lars, and burn their wooden images with fire....**

Deuteronomy 12:1-3

Why did God say the impure altars had to be destroyed?
*Whenever an individual participates at an impure altar, he is taking
into his life the seed of the motivations of those who are operating
that altar.* That seed will eventually be reproduced in him
unless God intervenes!

Impure altars defile the land by defiling the people. The
motivation behind the activity makes it pure or impure. You
can have two men trying to raise money for the same thing,
yet one can be pure and the other impure. The difference is
in the motivation of heart.

Professional *fund-raisers* brought into our churches generally bring manipulation and every unclean thing with them,
profiting off the people of God by getting a percentage of the
money they raise.

Any activity which requires the professional fund-raiser in
order to bring it to pass in the kingdom has all the earmarks of
being a man-made plan with the Holy Spirit nowhere involved.

Every dollar weaseled out of you by manipulation of any form is absolutely worthless as far as the covenant is concerned, and God is not obligated one whit to return it in any measure! In fact, what you are participating in is not a covenant blessing, but can be a covenant judgment!

Thank God, the Lord Jesus Christ is seated at the right hand of the Father extending grace to those of us who have been ignorant and out of the way. This is the promise that covers us when we are unaware of the con-job being perpetrated on us by the unscrupulous.

God in His love can, through blood-bought grace, bless us for our giving anyway.

A great assault is prophesied for the Church in the last days on the financial strongholds of the enemy. To be victorious in this season, we must be walking in God's covenant, standing firmly on His Word. We will never see these prophecies fulfilled if we remain ignorant and out of the way!

Recognize Manipulation

Several years ago, the Lord promised the day would come when the least-discerning saint would be able to recognize when manipulation is present. Deuteronomy 12:5 states:

> **But you shall seek the place where the Lord your God *chooses*, out of all your tribes, to put His name for His habitation: and there you shall go.**

The Hebrew root of the word for "habitation" is used for the abiding or settling of the glory cloud, signifying a time to stop and rest. Once again, God is going to reveal His glory and presence upon churches and ministries that are committed to pleasing Him. The glory cloud was a visible manifestation for all to see, recognizable by believers and unbelievers alike.

We have been conditioned to give by formula when there is apparent need. This is how ministries which are impure stay alive. *We have not taught the believers to get the voice of God and seek His face for direction on what to give where.*

Instead of teaching God's people their giving comes out of their relationship with the Lord, we have taught them giving by rote, rule, formula, and decree.

Tradition says ten percent belongs to the local church, and listen to God on your offerings, when the truth is you have to listen to God on *everything*! You have to listen to God about the amount of your offering and the distribution of your tithe. You have to listen to God about everything! It is only when you act on the voice of the Lord that you have the foundation to call forth covenant promises.

Take heed to yourself that you do not offer your burnt offerings in every place that you see;

but in the place which the *Lord* chooses....

Whose choice is it? It is God's choice! Look at verse 19:

Take heed to yourself that you do not forsake the Levite as long as you live in your land.

The very institution God ordained both to teach His people and to provide for the Levites has victimized them. Our current church tradition is the lingering fruit of the fulfillment of Acts 20:29-31:

For I know this, that after my departure savage wolves will come in among you, not sparing the flock.

Also from among yourselves men will rise up, speaking perverse things, to draw away the disciples after themselves.

Therefore watch, and remember that for three years I did not cease to warn everyone night and day with tears.

In many places, we have reduced the tithe to a formula, taken it for ourselves in the local assembly, and forsaken other Levitical ministries, bringing impurity to our altars and making the Word of God of none effect.

Deuteronomy 26 reveals covenant relationship to us through the tithe. A variety of teachers say tithing is Old Testament, not New, and therefore is not applicable to those of us who live in New Testament times. This conclusion is based on the assumption the tithe is a product of the Law, and it is true that the Law has been superseded by a New Covenant of grace.

In order to understand God's covenant, we must trace the tithe from its inception, which came more than four hundred years before the Law was ever instituted. The tithe was never instituted by the Law. The only thing the Law does for us is give insight into God's purpose and plan for the tithe. The Law itself does not apply concerning all of its different rules about the tithe today, but it does show us God's covenant purposes and plans.

We would do well to remember the old evangelical saying, "The New Testament is in the Old Testament concealed; the Old Testament is in the New Testament revealed."

The Tithe

Studying Old Testament laws as they relate to the tithe helps us draw parallels in our understanding of *why* God instituted the tithe, and why Hebrews 7 says Jesus still receives tithes today. The New Testament witnesses to the current reality of tithing as the foundation of God's covenant for blessing and provision for man.

In Deuteronomy 26:12, God held the individual, not the synagogue, responsible for distribution. Instead of teaching people to pray about distribution, we have institutionalized the tithe and taught the offering erroneously. God always intended the giving of tithes and offerings to come out of our relationship with Him. This means we have to pray, receive direction, and be willing to act on what God speaks and leads us to do by His Spirit.

> **When you have finished laying aside all the tithe of your increase in the third year, which is the year of tithing, and have given it to the Levite, the stranger, the fatherless, and the widow, so that they may eat within your gates and be filled,**
>
> **then you shall say before the Lord your God: "I have removed the holy tithe from my house, and also have given**

them to the Levite, the stranger, the fatherless, and the widow, according to all Your commandments which You have commanded me; I have not transgressed Your commandments, nor have I forgotten them.

"I have not eaten any of it when in mourning, nor have I removed any of it for any unclean use, nor given any of it for the dead. I have obeyed the voice of the Lord my God, and have done according to all that You have commanded me."

God expected His people to be able to look up to heaven and command the fulfillment of a promise. Verse 15 is explicit. The people were supposed to say to the Lord:

"Look down from Your holy habitation, from heaven, and bless Your people Israel and the land which You have given us, just as You swore to our fathers, 'a land flowing with milk and honey.'"

Commanding the Blessing

There is no way you and I can command the blessing God promised if we do not have a platform of obedience. In order to command the blessing of verse 15, the Jews had to obey the admonition of verse 14.

When we can clearly say to God, "I have obeyed your voice. I sent exactly what you spoke to me exactly where you said it should go," *then* we can call for the multiplication and the blessing God intended as a result of our being obedient in both tithe and offering.

By reducing tithe to a formula, we have separated God's people from any need to pray and hear the voice of the Lord. This removes the platform for realizing the promises of verses 17 and 18. Verses 17 and 18 (*KJV*) give us a foundation to stand before God and command a budget to be met:

Thou hast avouched the Lord this day to be thy God, and to walk in his ways, and to keep his statutes, and his commandments, and his judgments, and to hearken unto his voice:

And the Lord hath avouched thee this day to be his peculiar

people, as he hath promised thee, and that thou shouldest keep all his commandments.

The first time I read this in the *King James Version*, "avouched" flashed like a neon sign and I thought, "What in the world is an 'avouch'?" It must be important, because God promises if you can do it,

He will set you high above all nations which He has made, in praise, in name and in honour....

This promise is in the context of obeying the voice of God in distributing the tithe. You are going to be the head and not the tail, above and not beneath, if you can "avouch." God promises that He will set you not just above, but *"high above."*

Is the Church high above? Or are the unbelievers high above?

and that He will set you high above all nations which He has made, in praise, in name, and in honour, and that you may be a holy people to the Lord your God, just as He has spoken.

Being able to "avouch" is obviously the key to seeing God's promises in manifestation. But what does "avouch" mean? It is the Hebrew word *amar*.

According to *Gesenius' Hebrew Chaldee Lexicon to the Old Testament*, it is a *hiphel* verb. A *hiphel* verb is a causative verb. Causative means when you do what you are supposed to do, you cause happenings to take place as a result of your action.

Your activity sets in motion a chain of events which will cause a promise to come to pass, and all of heaven waits on you to initiate it by obeying God's word. This scripture says when you can pray and say, "God I have obeyed your voice," you cause God to do something.

Gesenius says, "Thou hast this day made Jehovah say, or promise, etc.; verse 18, 'And Jehovah hath made thee promise, i.e. you have mutually promised, and accepted, and ratified the conditions *of each other.'*"

59

The Lord led me to this passage in 1980. At that time, I had been in the radio ministry almost a year, and I felt led to go on a number of additional stations. This suddenly brought a dramatic increase in our monthly budget. The monthly radio bill was now equal to the budget for the rest of the ministry effectively doubling the monthly bills.

I was feeling the pressure. I prayed, "God where am I going to get the money to pay for the stations I believe You led me to go on?" My problem was not having the faith to operate at the new level of financial necessity.

The Lord led me to Deuteronomy 26, and the word "avouch" leaped off the page like a blinking, neon sign. When I discovered the causative covenantal meaning of "avouch," I knew I would never have to worry about a budget again, as long as I could look up to heaven and say, "Father, I have obeyed your voice!" Because it is a causative verb, it means when I take the time to pray, listen to Father's voice, and act on it, I cause Him to listen to my voice and respond to my need.

Gesenius' statement is amazing in its ramifications for every believer. He said, "You have mutually promised, and accepted and ratified the *conditions of each other.*"

Because I did what He told me to do, He will do what I ask Him to do. *Because I obeyed and gave where God told me to give, He will work and bring to pass what I tell Him I need.* This truth only works when I am obedient to the best of my ability, doing the whole counsel of God's will.

Free From Financial Pressures

This truth relieved me from all financial pressure! I knew regardless of how many stations God told me to go on, whether radio, TV, or whatever the project, I would never again have to worry about a budget as long as I obeyed. If the budget is not being met, either severe warfare has come, or I have to seek God about obedience.

When God has called you to head a ministry, and He brings more and more people on board, suddenly you are obligated for thousands of dollars in salaries, rental contracts, and so forth, with many people dependent on you. How do you walk in perfect peace in the middle of the financial pressure without yielding to manipulation, which is the temptation and tendency of so many?

Many of our Christian media programs are full of manipulation. The commercialization of the Gospel is at an all-time high. Everywhere we turn, we are being offered or sold something which is *guaranteed* to bring us a new level of blessing, peace, and joy. Merchandising God's Word, self-promotion, and advertising His gifts is an abomination!

When the foundation of an altar is impure, the truths taught there avail nothing, and the Body of Christ continues to struggle from day to day. We have inherited a system which is corrupt by tradition, but we live in a time-frame when God has promised to restore the foundations. He has promised prophetically a transfer of wealth to the Church for the purpose of a great end-time harvest; not for the purpose of individual blessing, and not for the purpose of making a name for ourselves, bathing in the glitz and the glory of personal pursuit.

Many pastors criticize traveling ministries for selling and manipulating in fund-raising, but they seldom realize the way they teach the tithe falls into the same category! The whole system has to be turned upside down in order for us to walk before God right side up.

The traditional way we have taught the tithe has removed the Biblical foundation for the individual believer's being able to stand before God and decree covenant blessing. God called those of us in leadership to be men and women who help open the windows of heaven, but in many cases, through tradition, we have closed them.

God will open the windows of heaven when leaders purify altars and walk in the way of His Word!

Chapter 6
The Spirit of Ammon

Nehemiah was called to bring restoration. He began his ministry during the reign of Artaxerxes I of Persia, 464-423 B.C. Queen Esther was Artaxerxes' stepmother and quite possibly was instrumental in Nehemiah's appointment as the king's cupbearer.

Nehemiah left Persia in the twentieth year of Artaxerxes' reign and returned in the thirty-second year, leaving again for Jerusalem after a few days. His heart was definitely in rebuilding Jerusalem.

His assignment was to help the restoration by rebuilding the walls and strengthening the people of the Lord. Nehemiah faced tremendous opposition, which came in stages. Nehemiah 2:9-11 outlines the first stage of his battle:

> **Then I went to the governors in the region beyond the River, and gave them the king's letters. Now the king had sent captains of the army and horsemen with me.**
>
> **When Sanballat the Horonite and Tobiah the Ammonite official heard of it, they were deeply disturbed that a man had come to seek the well-being of the children of Israel.**
>
> **So I came to Jerusalem and was there three days.**

Nehemiah first encountered the spirit of Ammon upon his return to Jerusalem. *The spirit of Ammon is absolutely opposed to any restoration and blessing God would like to bring to His people.*

Nehemiah laid out his purpose and gathered the Jews, exhorting them to rise up and build.

But when Sanballat the Horonite, Tobiah the Ammonite official, and Geshem the Arab heard of it, they laughed us to scorn and despised us, and said, "What is this thing that you are doing? Will you rebel against the king?"

So I answered them, and said to them, "The God of heaven Himself will prosper us; therefore we His servants will arise and build, but you have no heritage or right or memorial in Jerusalem."

Nehemiah 2:19,20

The foundation of the war had already been laid. Nehemiah declared his God-given purpose. The spirit of Ammon began to rise up in alliance with others to thwart God's plan. Once again Nehemiah had to say, "The God of heaven Himself will prosper us; we His servants will arise and build, but you have no heritage or right or memorial in Jerusalem." That was a very important statement!

But it so happened, when Sanballat heard that we were rebuilding the wall, that he was furious and very indignant, and mocked the Jews.

And he spoke before his brethren and the army of Samaria, and said, "What are these feeble Jews doing? Will they fortify themselves? Will they offer sacrifices? Will they complete it in a day? Will they revive the stones from the heaps of rubbish — stones that are burned?"

Now Tobiah the Ammonite was beside him, and he said, "Whatever they build, if even a fox goes up on it, he will break down their stone wall."

Hear, O our God, for we are despised; turn their reproach on their own heads, and give them as plunder to a land of captivity!

Do not cover their iniquity, and do not let their sin be blotted out from before You; for they have provoked You to anger before the builders.

So we built the wall, and the entire wall was joined together up to half its height, for the people had a mind to work.

Nehemiah 4:1-6

Nehemiah finished the first stage of what he was called to do in Jerusalem, and for a season he had to return to his position at court and report once again to the king. During the few years Nehemiah spent with the king; Tobiah, who was an Ammonite, began to find other ways he could hinder the restoration process in Jerusalem.

A man named Eliashib became High Priest in Jerusalem. Eliashib, along with the other priests, helped rebuild the Sheep Gate, according to Nehemiah 3:1. As High Priest he could assign chambers in the Temple to whatever purpose he pleased. Tobiah married into Eliashib's family and secured a position God never intended him to have.

> On that day they read from the Book of Moses in the hearing of the people, and in it was found written that no Ammonite or Moabite should ever come into the congregation of God,
>
> because they had not met the children of Israel with bread and water, but hired Balaam against them to curse them. However, our God turned the curse into a blessing.
>
> So it was, when they had heard the Law, that they separated all the mixed multitude from Israel.
>
> Now before this, Eliashib the priest, having authority over the storerooms of the house of our God, was allied with Tobiah.
>
> And he had prepared for him a large room, where previously they had stored the grain offerings, the frankincense, the articles, the tithes of grain, the new wine and oil, which were commanded to be given to the Levites and singers and gatekeepers, and the offerings of the priests.
>
> But during all this I was not in Jerusalem, for in the thirty-second year of Artaxerxes king of Babylon I had returned to the king. Then after certain days I obtained leave from the king,
>
> and I came to Jerusalem and discovered the evil that Eliashib had done for Tobiah, in preparing a room for him in the courts of the house of God.
>
> And it *grieved me bitterly*; therefore I threw all the household goods of Tobiah out of the room.
>
> Nehemiah 13:1-8

The spirit of Ammon had set itself up in the storerooms and completely controlled them. Balaam is a good example of one who yields to the spirit of Ammon. For honor and money he sold out and tried to curse the people whom God wanted to bless. Because God would not let him curse Israel, he sold Moab and Ammon a plan which would defile the covenant people!

The Moabites and Ammonites in return got victory over Israel, because Israel could no longer stand in their covenant, once impurity had a foothold. The covenant, would no longer work on their behalf; therefore, they could easily be conquered.

What was the fruit of Tobiah's new residence? It is clearly given in verses 9 and 10:

> **Then I commanded them to cleanse the rooms; and I brought back into them the articles of the house of God, with the grain offering and the frankincense.**

> **I also realized that the portions for the Levites** *had not been given them; for each of the Levites and the singers who did the work had gone back to his field.*

When Ministry Is Thwarted

When the spirit of Ammon gets involved in the storehouse, it will drive all the Levites out to their fields. No longer was the full flow of ministry God intended for His house available. When Tobiah, who represents the spirit of Ammon, controlled the storehouse, the Levites could no longer work together as God intended.

When Tobiah set up his home in the storehouse intended for the Levites, *the purpose and plan of God was immediately thwarted.* The Levites had to "work their own fields" or, in our vernacular, find a secular job, no longer devoting themselves to prayer and the ministry of the Word.

This was apparently the condition of the Early Church under the scribes and Pharisees. In Acts chapters 4 and 5, two different hearts are contrasted: one pure and one impure.

Barnabas is contrasted with Ananias and Sapphira as an example of what God is doing in the Church.

> Now the multitude of those who believed were of one heart and one soul; neither did anyone say that any of the things he possessed was *his own*, but they had all things in common.

Acts 4:32

When Tobiah set up his house in the storerooms, everything that came in, he said was *his own* to do with as he wants. But when the true heart of God is in manifestation, there is care one for the other, and recognizing the need of others supersedes personal ambitions. Acts 4:33-37 records:

> And with great power the apostles gave witness to the resurrection of the Lord Jesus. And great grace was upon them all.

> Nor was there anyone among them who lacked; for all who were possessors of lands or house sold them, and brought the proceeds of the things that were sold,

> and laid them at the apostles' feet; and they distributed to each as anyone had need.

> And Joses, who was also named Barnabas by the apostles (which is translated Son of Encouragement), a Levite of the country of Cyprus,

> having land, sold it, and brought the money and laid it at the apostles' feet.

Just as the Levites fled to their own land and were forced to make a living outside of God's intended purpose when Tobiah set up shop in the storehouse, so today the same fruit is seen in the New Testament. The spirit of Ammon is still alive and well!

The Levites were to wholly give themselves to God's Word, teaching and training the people, that there be no plague among the Israelites when they came into the Temple. But when the spirit of Ammon took over, the Levites were forced out. They had to go into their own jobs or till land God had intended only for grazing.

When Joshua conquered the land of Israel, the Levites were given cities and land for cattle, but they were told not to till the field, as the other Israelites did. The Levites' "produce of the field" was to come through the tithes of the people. Joshua 21:1-3:

> Now the heads of the fathers of the Levites came near to Eleazar the priest, to Joshua the son of Nun, and the heads of the fathers of the tribes of the children of Israel.
>
> And they spoke to them at Shiloh in the land of Canaan, saying, "The Lord commanded through Moses to give us cities to dwell in, with their common-lands for our livestock."
>
> So the children of Israel gave to the Levites from their inheritance, at the commandment of the Lord, these cities and their common-lands.

It would appear that Barnabas the Levite was forced to work a secular job because the system had degenerated to the place where it was much like what Nehemiah found upon his return to Jerusalem. Barnabas had to wait until God said, "Now is the time to quit your secular job, sell your land, plant the seed, and go into ministry. You have been called for years, but only now is the framework in place where you can be supported."

Another New Testament figure, Luke, was trained to be specific in his duties as a physician. It appears he was equally as precise in the words he chose as a writer. He used words like a mechanic uses tools.

Kho-ree-on is one of the two Greek words for "land" which generally indicates space, place, region, district, piece of land, a field, a city and its environs, i.e. the region around a city closely related economically and politically.

Ag-ros, on the other hand, according to *Bauers Lexicon*, is a plot of ground used mainly for agriculture, i.e. a farm. Weymouth, in his translation of Acts 4:37, says, "a farm." Vines denotes *ag-ros* as a field, especially a cultivated field; hence the country in contrast to town. Luke used *ag-ros*, not *kho-ree-on*, as one would expect if the land was being used in harmony with Levitical purpose.

The Greek word for "having" in verse 37 is *hoop-ar-kho*, "to begin below, to make a beginning, to come forth," giving us the indication that the beginning of Barnabas' ministry took place when he sold and then planted the seed from the field. *Ow-tos* of *ow-tos ag-ros* means "self" as used in all persons, genders, and numbers to distinguish a person or thing from or contrasted with another or to give emphatic prominence.

The Greek sentence structure makes prominent the fact that Barnabas sold *ag-ros*, not *kho-ree-on*. *Kho-ree-on* would tend much better to describe the kind of land Levites were to have according to God's plan, but the word used to describe what Barnabas had was *ag-ros*, indicating Barnabas was in the same position as the Levites Nehemiah found when he returned to Jerusalem.

Such is the fruit in any generation when the spirit of Ammon sets up his house in the Church! In Acts 4, when the money was laid at the apostles' feet, they did not use it solely for themselves. It was distributed to those who had need.

Defiling the Altar

There is an entirely different spirit at work in the Church which Jesus initiates. *The spirit of Ammon fully defiles an altar and turns it into a place of self-advancement, rule, and promotion.* Nehemiah had to kick Tobiah out and then cleanse what had been defiled! Nehemiah 13:11-13 states:

> So I contended with the rulers, and said, "Why is the house of God forsaken?" And I gathered them together and set them in their place.
>
> Then all Judah brought the tithe of the grain and the new wine and the oil to the storehouse.
>
> And I appointed as treasurers over the storehouse Shelemiah the priest and Zadok the scribe, and of the Levites, Pedaiah; and next to them was Hanan the son of

> Zaccur, the son of Mattaniah; for they were considered *faithful*, and their *task* was to *distribute* to their brethren.

Which spirit rules over the storehouse? Is there a dedication to distribute to the brethren and have the full flow of all five ministries functional and operational as soon as possible? Or is the commitment to build "me" a ministry? Luke 22:24-27 says:

> But there was also rivalry among them, as to which of them should be considered the *greatest*.
>
> And He said to them, "The kings of the Gentiles exercise lordship over them, and those who exercise authority over them are called 'benefactors.'
>
> "But not so among you; on the contrary, he who is greatest among you, let him be as the younger, and he who governs as he who serves.
>
> "For who is greater, he who sits at the table, or he who serves? Is it not he who sits at the table? Yet I am among you as the One who serves."

We serve people when we provide all the input they need to mature, equip them to accurately discern true from false, and fulfill God's call on their life. God never intended one man to do that by himself.

I believe the next move of the Spirit will be centered in the local church, but the spirit of Ammon will have to be prayed out first.

When we put money on an impure altar, God is not obligated one iota to return it! What is the motivation which governs the storehouse where you attend? Is it really a storehouse, or is it masquerading as a storehouse when, in fact, it is a dwelling place for Tobiah?

There are many men God has called to walk in five-fold ministry positions who are working secular jobs because Tobiah is living in the storehouse! If Tobiah is alive and well in your church, go to God in prayer and demand the purifying of the altar, and somewhere, somehow God will intervene!

Chapter 7
The Anointing To Spoil

Several years ago, the Lord posed these questions to me: "Son, how did I build my sanctuary? Where did my people get the money for the Tabernacle of Moses and for the Temple of Solomon? Did the money come from their jobs?"

I replied, "I don't know."

He said, "Well, find out."

That encounter initiated a search of scripture which changed my understanding of God's financial plan.

Exodus 12:35 and 36 says:

Now the children of Israel had done according to the word of Moses, and they had asked from the Egyptians articles of silver, articles of gold, and clothing.

And the Lord had given the people favor in the sight of the Egyptians, so that they granted them what they requested.

The Hebrew word translated favor is *khone,* which is a derivative of *khow-nan,* carrying the image of the strong and the weak in negotiation. The Egyptians, strong in military might and wealth, were weak when God began to move in behalf of His people. The last part of verse 36 says, "Thus they plundered the Egyptians."

When the Isralites came out of Egypt, God put an anointing on them. "They borrowed from the Egyptians." Whoever translated the Hebrew as "borrowed" had a sense of humor! They certainly did "borrow," but with no intention of ever giving it back! *They spoiled Egypt!*

This was my introduction to an aspect of God's plan I had never seen or understood before. The Lord said, "What about the Temple of Solomon?" There apparently has never been anything on the face of the earth that even approaches the value of the Temple Solomon built.

The image of the weak underdogs made strong through God's anointing and consequently taking what God wants them to have further develops and, perhaps, crystallizes, in First Chronicles 22, beginning in the first verse:

> Then David said, "This is the house of the Lord God, and this is the altar of burnt offering for Israel."
>
> So David commanded to gather the aliens who were in the land of Israel; and he appointed masons to cut hewn stones to build the house of God.
>
> And David prepared iron in abundance for the nails of the doors of the gates and for the joints, and bronze in abundance beyond measure,
>
> and cedar trees in abundance; for the Sidonians and those from Tyre brought much cedar wood to David.
>
> Now David said, "Solomon my son is young and inexperienced, and the house that is to be built for the Lord must be exceedingly magnificent, famous and glorious throughout all countries. I will now make preparation for it." So David made abundant preparations before his death.

How much did David prepare? More importantly, how did he get it? Verses 13 and 14 tell us:

> Then you will prosper, if you take care to fulfill the statutes and judgments with which the Lord charged Moses concerning Israel. Be strong and of good courage; do not fear nor be dismayed.
>
> Indeed I have taken much trouble to prepare for the house of the Lord one hundred thousand talents of gold and one million talents of silver, and bronze and iron beyond measure, for it is so abundant. I have prepared timber and stone also, and you may add to them.

The Open Bible, Expanded Edition has a footnote giving a formula for estimating the current value of these materials.

The gold was worth approximately $100.09 billion, while the silver amounted to a mere $21.84 billion. (Those values are based on $1000 per ounce. To get the current value, multiply market value accordingly.)

How did they get so much money? According to First Chronicles 26:26 and 27:

> This Shelomith and his brethren were over all the treasuries of the dedicated things which King David and the heads of fathers' houses, the captains over thousands and hundreds, and the captains of the army, had dedicated.
>
> Some of the *spoils* won in battles they dedicated to maintain the house of the Lord.

Building With Satan's Money

God's warriors received from Him an anointing to spoil, and out of that spoil His house was built! This is the second Temple built with the world's money. *God's buildings were built with Satan's money!*

Is the anointing to spoil really for today? Just because God released it for Israel in Egypt and through David's army does not mean it is for the New Testament Church. This was precisely my thinking when the Lord led me to Isaiah 53, the great prophetic glimpse of Jesus' ministry, verses 10-12:

> Yet it pleased the Lord to bruise Him; He has put Him to grief. When You make His soul an offering for sin, He shall see His seed, He shall prolong His days, And the pleasure of the Lord shall prosper in His hand.
>
> He shall see the travail of His soul, and be satisfied. By His knowledge My righteous Servant shall justify many, For He shall bear their iniquities.
>
> Therefore I will divide Him a portion with the great, And He shall divide the spoil with the strong, Because He poured out His soul unto death, And He was numbered with the transgressors, And He bore the sin of many, And made intercession for the transgressors.

This passage says Jesus bought and paid for an anointing to spoil He will parcel out in the last days. On this point, many scriptures agree, including the words of the Lord Himself. Matthew 12:28 and 29 say:

But if I cast out demons by the Spirit of God, surely the kingdom of God has come upon you.

Or else how can one enter a strong man's house and spoil his goods, unless he first binds the strong man? And then he will spoil his house.

The Greek word translated "spoil" in Matthew 12:28,29 is *dee-har-pad-zo*. It is the strengthened form of the root word *har-pad-zo* which, according to *Lexical Aids To The New Testament*, means "to strip, spoil or snatch, literally to seize upon with force," differing from *klep-to*, which means to steal secretly. It is an open act of violence in contrast to cunning, secret thieving.

Dee is an intensive, and is used to strengthen the force of the already strong word *har-pad-zo*. *Har-pad-zo*, without the strengthened addition of *dee*, appears in a very familiar passage, First Thessalonians 4:17:

And so shall we be caught up [*har-pad-zo*] together with the Lord and so shall we ever be with Lord.

Majoring in the Wrong Rapture

When we look at the force of the basic word used in First Thessalonians 4:17 for "rapture," versus the strengthened form used in Matthew 12:28 and 29, one truth quickly emerges: I believe many leaders over the last several decades have majored on the wrong rapture!

More authority and power will be released in the horizontal rapture than will be released in the vertical one. Many teachers have emphasized the Lord taking the Church out, when we should have emphasized the Church taking spoil away from the devil!

The *vertical* rapture will take care of itself. The *horizontal* one has to be done in the open. A brute display of force, not one done in secret, is the one we need to major on for the Church.

Jesus will display more *doo-nam-is* power and *ex-oo-see-ah* authority through the Church in the last days, destroying the works of the devil and bringing in an end-time harvest, than will be needed when He catches up the Church to meet Him in the air. Jesus personally divides the anointing to spoil with the strong. The first and primary fulfillment is Psalm 2, while the secondary is Isaiah chapters 60 and 61, both fitting together as pieces of the same puzzle.

Psalm 2:7-9 says:

> I will declare the decree: The Lord has said to Me, "You are My Son, Today I have begotten You.
>
> "Ask of Me, and I will give You the nations for Your inheritance, And the ends of the earth for Your possession.
>
> "You shall break them with a rod of iron; You shall dash them in pieces like a potter's vessel."

This aspect of the anointing to spoil deals with the harvest of souls which has to come from the nations. We should forget the Lord coming any day to take us out until we fulfill His revealed purposes. It is time to prepare for the greatest confrontation, persecution, and warfare the Church has ever known as we put our shoulder to God's purpose of bringing in a harvest of lost souls. How can we expect God to take us out when the greatest harvest ever, awaits?

Without the other aspect of the anointing to spoil, it is difficult to harvest souls. I am speaking of the fulfillment of Isaiah 60 and 61 as it relates to the Church.

Isaiah 60:1-5 says:

> Arise, shine; For your light has come! And the glory of the Lord is risen upon you.
>
> For behold, the darkness shall cover the earth, And deep darkness the people; But the Lord will arise over you. And His glory will be seen upon you.

The Gentiles shall come to your light, And kings to the brightness of your rising.

Lift up your eyes all around, and see: They all gather together, they come to you; Your sons shall come from afar, and your daughters shall be nursed at your side.

Then you shall see and become radiant, And your heart shall swell with joy; Because the abundance of the sea shall be turned to you, The wealth of the Gentiles shall come to you.

Isaiah 61:6,7 stresses God's commitment to fulfill His promises to the Church:

But you shall be named the Priests of the Lord, Men shall call you the Servants of our God. You shall eat the riches of the Gentiles, And in their glory you shall boast.

Instead of your shame you shall have double honor, And instead of confusion they shall rejoice in their portion. Therefore in their land they shall possess double; Everlasting joy shall be theirs.

Financing the Harvest

Prophetically, the Church has to bring in a harvest. This requires the releasing of a unique anointing in the last days. The harvest has to be financed, which, in turn, requires the release of another anointing. "The kingdom of God is upon us" means the rule, reign, and authority of Jesus Christ. We are commanded to occupy or, as *The New King James Bible* puts it, "do business" until the King comes! That business requires a progressive outpouring of the anointing to spoil!

I was on my way to conduct a Bible study meeting on a Tuesday night and suddenly the Spirit of God came upon me and I started to cry. I could hardly see the freeway. I was praying and weeping before God in a burst of intercession when suddenly out of my spirit came the interpretation: "God, if pastors won't support the fivefold ministry, give me the money and I will."

That night in the meeting, a businessman walked up and put a check for $18,000 in my hand!

I went out the next morning and took a check to a prophet of God. His wife had tears in her eyes and said, "This will be the first time since October (this occurred in March) of 1988 that we have been current in paying our bills."

And we wonder why the windows of heaven are not open to the Body of Christ! I thank God for revealing His heart to me through a visitation of the Holy Spirit. As a result of that experience, I began to make a commitment to use my faith for other ministries.

We do not want to be shepherds who care only about ourselves. A selfish financial attitude initiates a dangerous spiritual progression, according to Isaiah 56:10 and 11:

> **His watchmen are blind, They are all ignorant; They are all dumb dogs, They cannot bark; Sleeping, lying down, loving slumber.**
>
> **Yes, they are greedy dogs, Which never have enough. And they are shepherds who cannot understand; They all look to their own way, Every one for his own gain, From his own territory.**

We can safely say God will not release anything through altars dominated by such defiled hearts, which are continually looking for their own gain from their own quarter.

We are entering a season where using your faith more for others than self is required. God's heart is held in reserve for such yielded vessels!

I see in scripture a worldwide harvest prophesied for the last days in which every nation will hear God's word and respond. Where will the financing come from to underwrite this tremendous revival? Once again, the anointing will flow upon those chosen, and they will take their place like David, who prepared with five smooth stones to destroy the giant.

But where are we now?

Pure Altars Needed

Not only are the windows of heaven not open corporately, but the anointing to spoil is not flowing as it should individually in the Body of Christ. The anointing to spoil will be released through pure altars.

The flow depends on the heart of the one responsible for the ministry. This anointing will take the world's money to finance God's purposes and plans, not man's.

The same God who swept physical dictators from power to open the borders of Eastern Europe will sweep away spiritual dictators so the five smooth stones, signifying the five-fold ministry, can prepare the local Body.

This anointing brings with it a weighty responsibility. Some in David's army didn't want to share with those who stayed behind with the supplies, according to First Samuel 30:21-24:

> Now David came to the two hundred men who had been so weary that they could not follow David, whom they also had made to stay at the Brook Besor. So they went out to meet David and to meet the people who were with him. And when David came near the people, he greeted them.
>
> Then all the wicked and worthless men of those who went with David answered and said, "Because they did not go with us, we will not give them any of the spoil that we have recovered, except for every man's wife and children, that they may lead them away and depart."
>
> But David said, "My brethren, you shall not do so with what the Lord has given us, who has preserved us and delivered into our hand the troop that came against us.
>
> "For who will heed you in this matter? But as his part is who goes down to the battle, so shall his part be who stays by the supplies; they shall share alike."

Only when the heart of sharing and giving is established in an individual can he ever expect to qualify to receive God's anointing to move in the dimension of spoil. When God releases the anointing to spoil, we have the responsibility to dispense it accordingly. If your heart is not settled on this issue, you will never qualify for this anointing.

The anointing to spoil was bought and paid for at the

cross. Isaiah 53, which gives us great prophetic insight concerning what was accomplished there, says very clearly in verses 10 through 12:

> **Yet it pleased the Lord to bruise Him; He has put Him to grief. When You make His soul an offering for sin, He shall see His seed, He shall prolong His days, And the pleasure of the Lord shall prosper in His hand.**
>
> **He shall see the travail of His soul, and be satisfied. By His knowledge My righteous Servant shall justify many, For He shall bear their iniquities.**
>
> **Therefore I will divide Him a portion with the great, And He shall divide the spoil with the strong, Because He poured out His soul unto death....**

The prophetic word is very clear in outlining the fact that, while He was on the cross, Jesus accomplished and paid a price for this anointing to flow in the Body of Christ. He will see it come into manifestation in the last days, paying for the greatest revival the earth has ever seen.

Pastoring Your Business

In 1985 I was preparing for a marriage seminar in Washington, D.C. I went in the office on my day off to pray and ask the Lord about direction concerning what He wanted me to share during that marriage seminar. He would not speak one word to me about the marriage seminar, but began to talk instead about "pastoring your business." I knew it was a message for the Sunday morning prior to my flying to Washington, D.C.

I saw men who were gifted and called of God to a ministry which was every bit as important as standing in the pulpit. Yet their ministry was not a pulpit ministry. Their ministry was in the business world, and the Lord made me understand the concept of administering both was the same.

Businessmen were to begin to look at their businesses just as a pastor looked at his church! They were to pray for it, impart the vision to employees, receive the wisdom of God through intercession, and consequently face the same kind of resistance and warfare.

That encounter with the Lord produced a two-tape series entitled "Pastoring Your Business." It was one of about five events over a five-year period that God used to broaden my understanding, preparing me for ministry to businessmen.

In 1988 the Lord impressed me to hold my first Businessmen's Seminar. He instructed me to lay hands on people, planting and calling forth "the anointing to spoil." As I sought the Lord about the restoration of the anointing to spoil, I began to sense it, too, would be restored in reverse order.

When it first appeared in scripture, in Exodus 12, the whole body of believers participated. The second time we see it in scripture, it is not the whole body, but only a selective group. It is seen upon David's army as led by his mighty men. Once again this anointing will be given to those called, prepared, and selected by the Holy Spirit, given for examples to local bodies.

A few years after the Lord gave me the concept of "Pastoring Your Business," He spoke to me on the first day of my vacation to study Isaiah 23 and 24 in *The Living Bible*. Isaiah 23 in *The Living Bible* deals with the restoration of businesses which recognize their purpose of supporting ministry.

I knew this would be the selective group that we would first see moving in the anointing to spoil. Eventually, we will see a measure of it in the whole Body of Christ.

I personally have received the testimonies of businessmen who have put these principles into practice and seen God greatly multiply their ministries. One man shared that his business had grown in two years from five employees to one hundred and thirty-five. He initiated prayer meetings and healing services for his employees, and he said he spent a fair amount of his time just ministering to their needs.

He began to look at his business with the same attitude

toward helping and taking care of the people whom God sent to work there, as a pastor looks at his flock. He prayed for them, and was determined to serve them. God honored his heart to the extent that bankers were coming to offer credit lines because they saw the success he was enjoying! The secular world views the boss as one who must be served, but the Bible teaches the attitude of a servant is what qualifies you to be the boss. Success can come much more quickly when we change our attitude to agree with God's principle.

There is much God wants to do in the last days, and many ministries have to be supported. We are coming to a season when God is releasing the anointing to spoil, to take out of the world the money which is needed for the next great revival. This ministry is every bit as much a call of God as the call to stand behind the pulpit. It takes an anointing, just like ministering to a congregation. It takes a heart to serve and a willingness to obey the leadership of the Holy Spirit, just like serving a congregation.

Faithfulness Disregarded

The blind greed of some in corporate America has caused a curse to settle on their businesses that only restitution can remove. Firing people just prior to their qualification for vesting in pensions or other long-term corporate obligations, just to save the money, recklessly disregards years of faithful service.

Corporate raiders destroy years of hard work and earned goodwill with a ruthless motivation for profit, caring not about the lives they disrupt or careers they devastate.

God wants to raise up a standard in stark contrast to many in the current business climate. The anointing to spoil will be given to those who recognize their Biblical obligation to serve their employees and commit to act accordingly.

When God finds such committed hearts, there will be a supernatural transfer of business from the greedy to the gracious.

Where is your heart?

Chapter 8
Judging Righteous Judgment

Judging righteous judgment is one of the most difficult tasks facing believers in these times. There are always those who are quick to judge and blast everyone who does not measure up to the standard they feel appropriate. And yet, on the other hand, there are many who think it is absolutely too dangerous to make any judgments at all. This latter attitude is a by-product of taking Matthew 7:1-2 out of context:

> Judge not, that you be not judged. For with what judgment you judge, you will be judged; and with the same measure you use, it will be measured back to you.

On the surface, this passage seems to present an open and shut case, but on the other side of the proverbial coin is First Corinthians 5:11-13:

> But now I have written to you not to keep company with anyone named a brother, who is a fornicator, or covetous, or an idolater, or a reviler, or a drunkard, or an extortioner — not even to eat with such a person.

> For what have I to do with judging those also who are outside? Do you not judge those who are inside?

> But those who are outside God judges. Therefore "put away from yourselves that wicked person."

It is quite obvious from this passage that the Holy Spirit expects us to be a people who judge righteous judgment, yet the warning of Matthew 7 should ever be before us. To say we are to never judge within the Body, based on Matthew 7:1, is absolutely a perversion of scripture. It is not true. We are forced to make judgments within the Body of Christ.

What, then, is Matthew 7 dealing with? It is dealing with the proper attitude that enables us to judge righteous judgment. Matthew 7:3-5 says:

> And why do you look at the speck in your brother's eye, but do not consider the plank in your own eye?
>
> Or how can you say to your brother, "Let me remove the speck out of your eye"; and look, a plank is in your own eye?
>
> Hypocrite! First remove the plank from your own eye, and then you will see clearly to remove the speck out of your brother's eye.

The warning of Matthew 7 cannot be construed to say we never judge; rather, this is the criteria by which we approach making judgments within the Body.

Judging Ourselves

First, before we make declarations concerning the failure of others, we must seek the Lord to see if the presence of the same thing is in ourselves. To judge the local altar where you attend as impure, you must first ask God to show you the impurity in your own life. Then and only then can you approach judgment with the motivation of restoration and not from a position of hypocrisy, which demands God's judgment on you.

"Judge not, that you be not judged" is not a prohibition against making judgments concerning leadership or anyone else in the Body, as has been so prevalently taught, but rather is a warning to us about *how* we go about making such judgments.

Verse 4 says:

> ...how can you say to your brother, "Let me remove the speck out of your eye"; and look, a plank is in your own eye?

How easy it is to cause offenses when we make judgments because of a self-righteous attitude which exists due to our negligence in obeying this principle. To reach maximum effectiveness in bringing individuals to restoration through confrontation, we first must search our own hearts and let God show us the very same things in our lives that we have begun to see in the lives of others.

Then and only then can we approach people with compassion, because God has shown us where we have violated the same principle. To restore a brother, and remove sin from his life, we first must seek God to remove the same sin from our own lives.

Following these guidelines will help bring restoration rather than offense and destruction. God's purpose is to restore the Body, not destroy it.

If we would leave Matthew 7:1-12 in context, we would have no problem. In Matthew 6:1-4, Jesus said, "Give, but don't give like the hypocrites." In verses 5-15, He said, "Pray, but don't do it like the heathen." In verses 16-18, He said we should fast, but not like the hypocrites. Judging follows in the same context. We can judge, but if we judge as the hypocrites, God guarantees judgment in return.

Judgment is necessary, but it can only be done in the right spirit, when we judge ourselves first. God honors confronting errant behavior with compassion when the motivation is to restore!

We must remember one violation of any principle outlined in this book does not provide grounds for labeling the offender false or a counterfeit.

Selling the Anointing

Recently in Southern California, a nationally known minister promised a believer his prophetic anointing for a $50,000 donation, in exchange for his watch. The event was a fund-raiser for a local church, so the man did not apparently personally profit from the transaction.

The question remaining is, what becomes of the life of the donor when he realizes he gave $50,000, but got a $50.00 watch and a promise of anointing? Has that poor fellow been set up for shipwreck?

When can you judge a person a false prophet? We must realize good people sin! Just because a person sins does not mean he is false or counterfeit. When we see sin, we have a Christian obligation to confront, expecting repentance and restoration!

When a person refuses to accept our individual correction, we should take one other person with us who was involved, knows, or has seen the offense. When an individual refuses to accept the second witness and continues manipulating or offending, manifesting no evidence of repentance, then we can judge their work false or counterfeit.

Let he who is without sin cast the first stone!

Please don't make judgments about altars until you have first sought God to reveal impurity in your own life. Then and only then can you become part of the answer, rather than increasing the problem!

Chapter 9
Seeing God

Blessed are the pure in heart, for they shall see God.

Matthew 5:8

The apostolic understanding of this beatitude is perhaps best expressed in Hebrews 12:14:

Make every effort to live in peace with all men and to be holy. Without holiness no one will see the Lord.

At the risk of sounding theological, I want to quote one of the finest statements I've ever read concerning the single thread of both Matthew 5:8 and Hebrews 12:14. *The Expositor's Greek Testament* says of the promise of Matthew 5:8:

"shall see God": *ton the-on ops-on-tai:* their reward is the beatific vision. Some think the reference is not to the faculty of clear vision but to the rare privilege of seeing the face of the great King (so Fritzsche and Schange). "The expression has its origin in the ways of Eastern monarchs, who rarely show themselves in public, so that only the most intimate circle behold the royal countenance" (Schanz) = the *pure* have *access* to *the all* but inaccessible. (Italicized emphasis author's.)

I love the statement, "only the most intimate circle behold the royal countenance." This thought offers a concrete reason why some are seeing God in action while others are not!

There was a distinct difference between the ministry of Jesus and that of the scribes and Pharisees. The ministry of the apostles was recognizably different from that of the chief priests and elders of Israel.

God made it possible for the people to clearly distinguish between those serving dead tradition and those serving God. You could easily *see* the difference! In John 14 (*NIV*), Philip asked:

Lord, show us the Father and that will be enough for us.

Jesus answered in verses 9-12:

"Don't you know me, Philip, even after I have been among you such along time? Anyone who has seen me has seen the Father. How can you say, 'Show us the Father?'

"Don't you believe that I am in the Father, and that the Father is in me? The words I say to you are not just my own. Rather, it is the Father living in me, who is doing his work.

"Believe me when I say that I am in the Father and the Father is in me; or at least believe on the evidence of the miracles themselves.

"I tell you the truth, anyone who has faith in me will do what I have been doing. He will do even greater things than these, because I am going to the Father."

Blueprint for Ministry

There was never a sharper blueprint for ministry than what we see here! Jesus made it very clear to the disciples that His mission was to demonstrate God. If He obeyed the leadership of the Holy Spirit, people would see God. That was not just a one-time statement about His personal life, but a principle which would govern effective ministry. The Church should be demonstrating the Father. Unbelievers should see God working and living through us.

What was the difference between Jesus and the scribes and Pharisees? He taught and ministered *as one who had authority*. Demons were subject to Him. Sickness and disease had to bow and flee at His command.

We live in a dying world that is filled with unbelievers. Some are going to hell because, instead of seeing God in us, they see competition in the Church, misappropriation of funds, begging for finances on television and radio, manipulation, selling, profiteering from the Gospel, and believers suing each other in court!

We are called to demonstrate God's authority in the earth. Jesus made this very clear in John 14:12

...he who believes in Me, the works that I do he will do also....

When will the world see God operating in the Church? When purification comes to our altars. *Our effectiveness in spiritual things is determined by the purity of our hearts before God.*

The Word ministered or shared out of a pure heart comes forth with clarity and impact that can be achieved no other way. The prayer prayed by the leadership of the Spirit out of a pure heart is assured an answer. John 14:13,14 (*NIV*) says:

And I will do whatever you ask in my name, so that the Son may bring glory to the Father. You may ask me for anything in my name, and I will do it.

Many prayers are prayed that do not receive answers. Could it be because they are prayed out of something less than a pure heart?

A Righteous Gentile Is Honored

Cornelius is an example of a man who was visited supernaturally. The Bible is not silent about why! What he did came from a pure heart. Both his prayers and his giving came before God as a memorial, which shows us that whenever something comes out of a pure heart, God notices, hears, and responds accordingly.

An angel was dispatched to Cornelius with very specific instructions. He was told to contact Peter, and he was given detailed instructions on how to find the house where Peter was staying.

Just as the visit to Cornelius was supernatural, so was God's moving on Peter to prepare him to step beyond tradition and minister to the Gentiles. When Cornelius' messengers arrived, Peter was ready to accompany them, because God had given him the same vision three times.

The Holy Spirit even told Peter three men were looking for him and to go downstairs without hesitating and go with them, for "I have sent them." Why did God choose Cornelius for a mighty visitation and to be the first Gentile filled with the Holy Spirit? Do you suppose it was because of his pure heart?

How many people will God use us to bring into the kingdom if we will but walk before Him in purity! If we allow the Holy Spirit to purify us through His revealed Word, we can expect to see God in manifestation through us.

What Financial Pressure Reveals

This seems to be a season in the Body of Christ when many are under financial pressure. If we point our finger at impurity in our corporate altars as the sole reason, we will greatly err! We should *first* look in the mirror and ask God if perhaps He is trying to reveal the effects of the spirit of mammon at work in our individual lives.

Different Gospels record Jesus addressing this issue: "You cannot serve God and money." How much trust have we put in the material things of this world? Our culture is shot through with materialism, and often it seems the spirit of mammon dominates the desires of God's people. When financial pressure arises, we are confronted with our own lusts, wrong desires, and undetected trust in material things. It is painful when God deals with us in this way, but it certainly is effective!

Financial pressure can quickly reveal attitude of heart. We can learn that the things we thought were necessary for our well-being and happiness are not needed at all! The spirit of mammon has some unique manifestations which need to be considered. It can cause an individual to give for the wrong reasons and to give to the wrong place without seeking God's wisdom or direction. It usually manifests itself through impure motivation.

It seems at times people are trying to manipulate God through giving. We do that by *giving in order to get*. Our reasoning generally misapplies some of the things we have been taught. We find the promise of a thirty-, sixty-, and hundred-fold return, so we begin to give with a motivation for a thirty-, sixty-, or hundredfold return. Soon we find ourselves giving in order to receive. "I'll give so much into this ministry, and I am claiming a certain return; therefore, I can expect God to give me back a certain amount, or to give me what I need."

God does promise that He will give back to us, but there is a heart attitude which must reflect His! If we look at Jesus as the example, John 3:16 says, "God so *loved* that He gave...." Ephesians 5 says we are to "...imitate God as well beloved children imitate their father."

The motivation of God's heart for giving Jesus was love. If our giving comes out of a pure heart, we can certainly expect a return! But have we crossed the line? Are we subtly giving because we want a specific return? We need to examine our motivation for giving.

Some people who are wealthy give with the intention of exerting control on the church leaders. This financial pressure can be applied in a variety of ways to influence decisions made concerning the church or ministry.

Giving With Strings Attached

I was told of a man who loved to sing out of a hymnal, but the worship leader only used spontaneous songs in praise and worship. This contemporary style of praise and worship violated the rich man's favorite tradition. He promised to give the church a large sum if they would buy his favorite hymnals.

What pastor could pass up a $100,000 gift, especially when they only have to spend a small percentage to satisfy the giver? The motivation of the giving was obvious. The problem was, the leadership needed the money. They began to reason, "What can it hurt? Let's go ahead and buy the hymnals. We don't have to use them very often." But when somebody gives $100,000 to your church for buying hymnals, you'd better believe there will be pressure to use them.

There is certainly nothing wrong with hymnals. This is just one example of how manipulation can motivate giving. Those of us who stand in leadership positions really need to seek God for wisdom as to how to handle such situations. Receiving money into your ministry tainted by impure motivation can bring impurity into the corporate altar.

Another form of manipulation comes through people who are helped through a ministry. They decide that the pastor or the prayer team, rather than the grace of God, is responsible for their blessing! They continue to give solely with the expectation, hope, and sometimes pressure, for church leadership to do their personal spiritual warfare. In effect, they are buying your time.

At that point, if a leader continues to receive their money, it is no longer the Holy Spirit who is guiding the prayer time, but an obligation to pray consistently for the one who is giving!

I know of one pastor who was told by the Holy Spirit the church could not keep any of the money given by a person over a period of time. He was instructed to give all the money back. The pastor said, "Because the money was given out of a wrong motive, we could not keep any of it in the ministry. Any of the money kept would have had a polluting effect upon the ministry."

Some people give into ministries in order to be noticed and considered for leadership positions. The deacon's ministry has probably been bought more than any other! Sometimes the motivation is ambition; other times, recognition or the desire to have an opportunity to minister.

There are many great promises of God that show us His desire to multiply and return what we give. Nevertheless, we really need to check our heart and make sure our motivation is pure. Then and only then are we going to see the Lord move in the financial realm. Isaiah prophesied we would see Him!

Some people come under financial pressure simply because of disobedience. We cannot go out and blindly buy everything we want and expect God to bless it. We are really servants of the Lord, and we must submit our decisions to the Holy Spirit. When we buy things we want but God has not instructed us to get, He has no obligation to pay for them.

When I was in seminary, one of the things we were taught which made a strong impression on me was, "What God tells you to do, *He* pays for. What you decide to do on your own, *you* pay for." I have met many people in the Body of Christ who are under financial pressure strictly because of disobedience. Usually large items are involved, such as a house, car, recreational vehicle, boat, or something else which was not necessarily needed.

How and When To Receive

Manipulation is as dangerous as disobedience. As I was finishing this book and getting ready for a trip to the Midwest, our air-conditioner went out the day before I left. During the course of doing local Bible studies every week for twelve years, I had met a wonderful Christian family whose business is air-conditioning. I called the man and he agreed to drop by my house and look over the unit. I knew it needed to be replaced because of some previous work.

The next day I left for the Midwest with the understanding that it was to be replaced with one of equal capacity. He replaced both heating and air-conditioning units, and when I got home I called him to get the cost. He said he and his wife had prayed about it, and decided they wanted to give the unit into our ministry.

In the first place, they would not have been giving it to the ministry; they would have been giving it to me personally.

Second, I didn't feel in my heart I could accept that gift. The reason was, I had initiated the contact. Had the Holy Spirit initiated the chain of events, then I could have received it. Had that man called me by the leadership of the Holy Spirit and said, "The Lord told me you need a new heating and air-conditioning unit, and I'm supposed to give it to you," then I could have received it. But because I called him and asked him to come out and look at the unit, I was the one who initiated the activity. Therefore, to have received it from him would have been to take advantage of a good-hearted brother, which is all too common in ministry!

When I shared that principle with him on the phone, he related to me two incidents where he felt he had been taken advantage of. He was overjoyed at my stand. His business activity had been down, and he really didn't feel like he could afford to do that for me, yet he and his wife wanted to with all their heart. Those of us in leadership need to realize that the saints long to bless and give to us, but there is a standard of integrity that we need to raise up concerning how we deal with the people we minister to.

I want to see God in my life and ministry! I know for that to happen, I must maintain a level of integrity where my own heart does not in any way condemn me when I go before God in prayer. When I pray from a pure foundation, I know I am going to receive what I am asking for, as long as I am asking in the will of the Father.

The reason I could turn down the offer for the heating and air-conditioning unit was because of a much smaller incident that happened early in my ministry. There was a man attending my Bible studies who owned an auto parts store. I needed a battery at one point, so I decided to give him the business. I went into his store and got the battery I needed, and in the process he said, "I want to give you this battery." I told him I wanted to pay for it, but he said, "No, I want to give you this battery." So I took the battery, even though I had gone to see him to buy one.

The Disappearing Donor

After about two weeks, I never saw that man again in my Bible study. As I prayed about the situation, I felt like the Lord showed me, this man began to look at me as falling into a common category with so many others, willing to take advantage of any situation. At that point, I began to pray about God's necessary standard for dealing with saints who own their own businesses.

I believe integrity demands that what we as ministers of the Gospel initiate with Christian brothers and sisters in business, we pay for! When the Holy Spirit initiates something, however, what they want to give can be received with rejoicing and thanksgiving.

But when we initiate the contact with Christian business people, it is incumbent upon us to pay for what we get. Only then are there good feelings on both sides, and when the day comes you need their services again, you can ask with a clear conscience.

"Blessed are the pure in heart, for they shall see God." Jesus said, "The works that I do will you do also and greater works than these will you do because I go to the Father."

I believe we are rapidly approaching a season when God demands to be seen in the lives of every believer. The key to God's being seen is clear. It requires purity of heart, motivation, thought, and action.

Hebrews says we can "...come boldly to the throne of grace and obtain grace and mercy in a time of need." We need to remember "...that only the most intimate circle behold the royal countenance. The pure have access to the all but inaccessible."

As the Lord leads us to ever greater heights of purity and accountability, we can expect His visible manifestation. Multitudes of unbelievers will have to acknowledge they *see* God at work in the Church! Then and only then will the great end-time harvest come forth.

Once again, God is waiting on us!

Books and Tapes Available By Grace Through Faith

ALL WORD AT WORK MINISTRIES materials are offered on a "pray and obey" basis. We believe Second Corinthians 8:9-15 should govern book and tape distribution: "...that now at this time your abundance also may supply their lack, that their abundance also may supply your lack — that there may be equality."

The Word of the Lord should be available to all who desire it without ever turning anyone away because of a lack of finances. To make that possible, those who can afford it must be sensitive, indeed, recognizing the Lord probably will ask them to support those who cannot!

Because the initial investment of production costs is shouldered by WORD AT WORK MINISTRIES, we limit the number of tapes by mail to one series or eight singles, and one each of the books per month. This policy was initiated by the leadership of the Holy Spirit and can be suspended individually or corporately as He directs.

All believers receiving books, tapes, and Bible studies from this ministry agree to read Second Corinthians 8:9-15 and act accordingly! God blesses those who respond in integrity.

We encourage the copying of Bible studies and duplication of tapes to share with others, but forbid it for sale or lending where fees are involved.

Books, tapes, and Bible studies are mailed according to availability of funds.

Tape Series

AN EXAMPLE OF TEAM MINISTRY I-III. A demonstration of Holy Spirit freedom every pulpit should enjoy.

AFTER GOD'S OWN HEART I-IX. An in-depth look at the Fivefold Ministry of Ephesians 4, what each contributes, and how to recognize them according to the measure of God's heart assigned to their specific office.

BUYING FROM GOD I-IV. Presents an understanding of the spiritual principles that relate to the effective use of our time.

CLEANSING THE TEMPLE I-IV. Purity precedes power.

DISCERNING MINISTRIES I-VI. Guidelines for discerning the evil from the counterfeit.

EXCEPT THE LORD BUILD THE HOUSE I-III. How God qualifies and promotes people.

FAITH, A BY-PRODUCT OF? I-III. A study of the necessity of obedience.

FULLNESS I-IV. This principle is the key to what must happen in winding up the age.

GETTING GOD'S HEART I-IV. The second series to listen to after *Purifying the Altar.* How to develop servanthood.

HOW GOD PREPARES PEOPLE FOR MINISTRY I-IV. Adversity is the crucible for maturity.

KNOWING AND UNDERSTANDING GOD I-III. A study of those characteristics which form a foundation for fellowship between personalities of like mind.

KNOWING THE TIMES AND SEASONS I-IV. Identifies the changing criteria as we transition to a third leadership generation in this century and what to expect in the future.

LEARNING OBEDIENCE I-IV. A study of Jesus fulfilling God's will, as a parallel to completing our assignments.

MARKED MEN I-II. How to recognize the divine mark.

PASTORING YOUR BUSINESS I-II. Strictly for those called to the business world. Identifies the attitude necessary for treating your business as God sees it: a ministry.

PERSEVERANCE I-IV. The most important ingredient in the final stages of the birthing process.

PREPARING FOR PERSECUTION I-IV. In April 1986 the Lord said, "Prepare my people for persecution."

PROPHETIC SURVEY I-VIII. A look at the Church and where it stands today versus where God wants to take it.

PURIFYING THE ALTAR — PART II. A look at personal relationships and how they affect the return on our giving.

RECOGNIZING OPEN DOORS I-II. Identifies the hidden opportunities God sends and helps us discern accordingly.

RECRUITING TRUE WARRIORS I-III. A call to intercession and standing in the gap, that judgments slated for this nation might be stopped.

SEVEN "KAIROS" OF THE NEXT "CHRONOS" I-IV. An in-depth look at some of the fingerprints of God expected to come during the next forty years.

SPIRITUAL AUTHORITY I-VIII. A look at why those who have it, have it, and why those who don't, don't.

THE ANOINTING TO SPOIL '88 I-IV. The very first Business Seminar done with the laying on of hands, setting apart those who have been called to minister in this area.

THE ANOINTING TO SPOIL '89 I-III. An entirely different approach to the anointing to spoil, based on what we learned from '88.

THE ANOINTING TO SPOIL '94 I-III. God brings captivity and brokenness to those He intends to use greatly.

THE BLOOD OF JESUS I-V. It was shed in four different places, each one redemptive, each one special, and each one necessary as an equipping for our warfare.

THE CHARACTER OF AN INTERCESSOR I-IV. Outlines the platform that makes prayer work.

THE COST OF BUYING & SELLING THE GOSPEL A&B. What the Bible says about merchandising in all its forms.

THE COST OF THE PARTY I-III. Ramifications of the Toronto Blessing and why God chooses the bizarre.

THE "MARTUREHO" OF GOD I-II. God gives a witness to those who please Him. Without that witness we cannot really stand.

THE TRIUMPHAL ENTRY I-IV. This series is a prophetic look at Jesus entering Jerusalem for the last time with accompanying parallels to His moving again in our era.

THREE KEYS TO THE UPPER ROOM I-VII. Seven chapters in scripture were devoted to what took place in the Upper Room. It is a place of preparation for moving in the Holy Spirit in the last days.

WARFARE IN WORSHIP I-III. Many times in a worship service we have the opportunity to go into spiritual warfare, but do not take it because of tradition.

WHAT IS FAITH? I-VIII. An in-depth study of how to stand Biblically and believe God Biblically.

WHEN GOD VISITS I-IV. Jesus is coming *to* the Church before He comes *for* it, and this outlines what we can expect in the process.

WHEN IS CHURCH, *CHURCH*? I-VIII. An expose of the real versus the counterfeit.

Tape Singles

A HEART FOR RESTORATION

A RELIGIOUS SYSTEM INHERITED

AN OFFERING IN RIGHTEOUSNESS

APPLYING THE CROSS

DEVELOPING ENDURANCE

DIVINE VISITATIONS

EZEKIEL 7:19

FREEDOM THROUGH FORGIVENESS

GETTING GOD'S PRIORITIES

HAVE YOU *REALLY* FORGIVEN?
HOW BIG IS YOUR GOD?
HOW SHALL I KNOW?
HOW TO DEAL WITH EVIL
HOW TO HANDLE PRESSURE
HOW'S YOUR HEDGE?
JUDGEMENT
LOVE THAT PURIFIES
MANY ARE CALLED BUT FEW ARE CHOSEN
MUTUAL SUBMISSION
PATHWAY TO PROMOTION IN CAPTIVITY
PRIMARY APPLICATION OF MARK 11:23-24
PRINCIPLES OF JUDGEMENT
PUTTING SATAN UNDER FOOT
RECONCILIATION
SEPARATION: GOD'S PREPARATION
SEVEN LEVELS OF OBEDIENCE
SPIRITUAL PREJUDICE
THE BIT AND BRIDLE GENERATION
THE CHANGING OF THE GUARD
THE COST TO BIRTH A REVIVAL
THE DOUBLE PORTION
THE GREATEST FAITH OF ALL
THE PRINCE HATH NOTHING IN ME
THE WILL, WAYS, AND TIMING OF GOD
THREE KINDS OF STORMS
THREE KINDS OF VISITATIONS
THREE PRINCIPLES THAT WIN WARS
THREE STAGES OF REPENTANCE
THREE VEILS

UPHEAVAL IN THE CHURCH
WARFARE AT THE SECOND FRONT
WE HAVE PRAYED FOR REVIVAL BUT WE ARE GETTING?
WHEN GOD GOES ON VACATION
WHEN GOD IS ASHAMED
WHEN THE HOLY GHOST TAKES OVER
WHERE DO YOU SIT?
WHO WILL YOU PLEASE?
WHOLLY TRUSTING GOD

Books

THE BLESSINGS OF DILIGENCE will show you how to develop characteristics that bring God's blessings.

POWER OF AGREEMENT will teach you how to fulfill your part so the Father can perform His promise.

Daily Bible Study

The *Word At Work* is a daily Bible study mailed monthly dealing with topical subjects usually corresponding to current messages.

About the Author

Al Houghton grew up in a small town in Missouri. He graduated from the University of Missouri at Columbia, with a Bachelor of Science Degree in Marketing. After graduation, he joined the Navy to become a pilot, flying one hundred and sixty-one combat reconnaissance missions during the Vietnam War. He left the military to fly commercially, but God dramatically intervened calling him into ministry.

In 1975, he moved to Southern California to attend seminary and earned a Master of Divinity Degree in theology. Immediately upon graduation, the Lord instructed him to start a teaching ministry and live by faith.

The teaching ministry began in home Bible studies, but grew to occupy other facilities, like Mott Auditorium on the campus of the U.S. Center for World Missions in Pasadena, where Al taught for ten years.

1984-'87 marked a transition as God added a prophetic touch to the teaching ministry. Doors opened in other nations and Al began to minister at International Leadership Conference.

A daily Bible study, entitled the "Word at Work," was published and is available upon request.

Al has authored three books, *Power of Agreement*, *The Blessings of Diligence*, and *Purifying The Altar*. *Purifying The Altar* will soon be available in French and Spanish.

Al resides in Yorba Linda, California, with his wife, Jayne, and their children, Jonathan, Julie, and Michael.